PRAISE FO  .D

"In Forgiving Stephen Redmond, a corpse in a wall kicks off a mystery that crackles with sharp dialogue and an insider's view of a quickly disappearing part of Manhattan."
—*Richie Narvaez, author of Noiryorican*

"A gripping opening plunges the reader into a story of colliding cultures that never goes where expected. Sidransky creates an array of strong, vivid, authentic characters to resolve a mystery that plays out across decades in the Washington Heights neighborhood he clearly loves. My heart and my head kept me turning pages. A great read."
—*Jane Kelly, author of the Meg Daniels Mysteries*

"The crime drama, at the heart of the plot, was well-developed and well-paced. It kept me guessing to the very end. The historical detail and various subplots interweave to create a compelling read. I highly recommend this book."
—*Heidi Slowinski, author of The House on Maple Street*

FORGIVING STEPHEN REDMOND

A. J. Sidransky

A Black Opal Books Publication

DEDICATION

For Juan Carlos Gonzalez,
who always sought the truth.

FOREWORD and ACKNOWLEDGMENTS

When I wrote Forgiving Máximo Rothman, I intended it to be a stand-alone work. But, as early in the process as my writer's workshop, my fellow writers insisted that the characters had legs. I still didn't intend a series. When I began speaking to groups about the book, I often got questions about the loose ends I had left. I should say honestly that was done completely on purpose, with no intention of tying them up. Eventually, I too felt the characters had more to say. The result was my second book, Forgiving Mariela Camacho, which examined the experience of Dominican immigration, and the continuing themes of the relationship between fathers and sons, and substitute-fathers and sons, as well as the minefield of male friendship.

With the completion of Mariela, I realized one more volume was necessary to examine the remaining issues put forth in Forgiving Máximo Rothman. For those who have not read Forgiving Máximo Rothman, be aware that there are some spoilers in Forgiving Stephen Redmond, but even so, I believe you will find all three compelling, even if read out of sequence. My apologies for not writing them in order. Sometimes the muse is just upon you. If you are starting the series now, read Máximo first, Stephen second, and Mariela third. As to Kurchenko and Gonzalvez, they may come back some day, but the story of Máximo and his family and friends, and Sosúa, is done.

I have plenty of people to thank for their help in the writing and publishing of this book. First and foremost is Antonia Mejia Torres, grandmother of Charlie D. Soto, who very generously agreed to speak with me about the experiences of her family under the Trujillo regime. In this time of the potential arrival of autocracy and fascism in our own country, we need to pay attention to the past, particularly the past of others who have experienced similar events. Trujillo was a racist, a rapist, and a crime boss. Sound familiar? We see a comparable type personality in control of our government today. I don't use his name, ever. But, unlike the Dominican Republic of 1960, we still have a functioning democracy, though an injured one. Let's not let the situation come to the point where an assassination is necessary to right the course of our great democracy.

I have dedicated this book to my dear friend, Juan Carlos Gonzalez. Born in the Dominican Republic, he came to the United States as a teenager. He achieved the American dream, an education, a family, a career, a life of service to his community. He was one of the finest people I have ever known. He left us much too soon in November of 2018, in a shocking moment. He is loved and he is missed. He was pure of heart and like the protagonists in this book, he always sought the truth for its own sake. May his memory be a blessing.

Many others deserve mention here. Let me start with my editor and publisher, Susan Humphreys and Black Opal Books, for having the confidence in me to publish this book. Thanks also to Henry and Tehila Reiser for reading the manuscript and providing great feedback. Thanks to Led Black his many years of guidance and encouragement, and also for reading the manuscript, and to my first and foremost fan, Joan Silver Ayoub, who always gives me an honest opinion.

Thanks, as always to my wife, Hope, and my son, Jake, for their continued support and love, and to my cousin Fred Miller, who props me up when I start to think I can't write.

Then there's my brotherman, William Cruz. That's his name for me. I couldn't ask for a better friend. You are my brother from another mother, Pete to my Tolya, Pete through and through; honest, direct, and full of love. I wrote him for you, in all three books. The truth is, if you hadn't brought me to Santo Domingo, these books never would have been written.

A. J. Sidransky
March 1, 2019

Prologue
Washington Heights, NYC
5 July 1966
3:00 a.m.

Hands worked deftly applying plaster to lathe. With each application the face of the dead man receded a bit more into darkness, never to be seen or heard from again. The plasterer found that thought satisfying. This criminal didn't deserve the propriety of remembrance. His name would be blotted out, forever erased from memory.

At the same time an ache settled into the plasterer's soul, one that he knew would never leave him. He'd gotten what he wanted, but it didn't feel right. It didn't feel the way he'd expected it to feel. How empty, how devoid of satisfaction this revenge was. Not at all what he'd imagined. He'd planned it out, choreographed it like a ballet, but in the end, the dance took on a life of its own. The story wrote its own ending.

Before placing the last lump of plaster on the wire mesh, the plasterer stared at the face inside one final time. Unexpectedly, though he recognized the face in death, it was in some way different than in life. In life, this face had been calculating, self-important, overly confident. In death it appeared confused. It would wear this expression for eternity. With all its cockiness, it never saw what was coming, and when death came this face was shocked, and would remain so forever.

The plasterer spread the last of the wet, sandy, putty-like mortar over the fine mesh encasing the dead man forever. He smoothed it out, the wall becoming whole again. Tomorrow he would paint the entire room. His stomach turned a bit, as if he were about to vomit, but there was nothing in it to expel. He hadn't eaten in hours. He kept the dry heave at bay, straightened himself up and stretched his arms high into the air and behind his head, bits of half-dry plaster flying off his cloths and hair. Memory overwhelmed him, yet there was no satisfaction. Even this was not enough. But it would have to be. The dead were buried now, both here and in Santo Domingo. Life would go on. Perhaps he would too, if he could only learn to forgive himself.

Chapter 1

The heat slapped Detective Tolya Kurchenko in the face as he pushed open the door from Mi Ranchito Restaurant onto Saint Nicholas Avenue. No matter how many years he lived in Washington Heights, no matter how many years passed since leaving Russia, he would never get used to the heat and humidity of a New York summer.

"*Pana*," said his partner, Detective Pete Gonzalvez, rubbing his bare arms with both hands, "it's too cold in that restaurant. And I don't know what you like about Mexican food, anyway. Tomorrow we're gonna find some good Dominican lunch."

"Sure, whatever you say," Tolya replied, smiling to himself. Pete was a creature of habit. He could eat the same thing every day, at the same table, at the same place. Unfortunately for Pete, the Dominican hash house they ate at virtually every day for years had closed, soon to be an upscale steak house. Another reminder of the changing neighborhood.

Tolya followed Pete to the corner of 184th Street. "Let's cross here," Pete said, still rubbing his arms.

"No, walk with me, I gotta go up the block to Mi Pais. Karin asked me to pick up some platanos maduros, and some yuca."

"Okay," Pete replied. "I need to warm up anyway before we go back to the station, too cold in there too." Pete punched Tolya playfully on the left arm. "She's turned you into a real Dominicano?"

"I guess," said Tolya. He chuckled to himself. The truth was he wasn't ever sure what he was, how to define himself.

As they entered Mi Pais market at the corner of 185th Street and St Nicholas Avenue Tolya's cell phone rang, the unique ringtone indicating it was their captain. Tolya put it on speaker.

"Where are you boys?"

"Coming back from lunch."

"Where exactly?"

Tolya looked at Pete. "St. Nick and 185th."

"Picking up a few things for the wife for dinner?"

Tolya didn't respond.

"Take me off the speaker."

Tolya touched the screen and placed the phone to his ear. "Swing by the construction site on 187th between Wadsworth and Broadway," the captain said. "We just got a call. They found a body in the building."

The three wood frame houses on the north side of West 187th street between Broadway and Wadsworth Avenue, stood hanging on the side of the steep hill for some seventy years. They had been vacant for as long as Tolya could remember. Now they were finally coming down, to be replaced by a new luxury apartment building, the other half of the change in the neighborhood.

While the Dominican community centered around St. Nicholas Avenue was thinning out, replaced by newly arrived Mexican immigrants—a fact Pete was constantly complaining about—the Russian immigrants, old German ladies, orthodox Jews, and the aging, retired teachers and civil servants that formed the white community west of Broadway was becoming younger, richer, and more hip.

Washington Heights was the 'last frontier' in Manhattan. What was more significant, the line between the white community west of Broadway and the Latino community east, was blurring. Luxury apartments east of Broadway geared to these refugees from lower Manhattan and Hipster Brooklyn were now a fact of community life.

"Excuse me." Tolya shouted to the crowd of construction workers huddled in front of the entrance to the site. He and Pete waved their badges, as they slogged down the hill from its crest at Wadsworth Avenue. Beads of sweat dripped from Tolya's neck down his back. Tolya glanced over at Pete. As always, the heat didn't seem to affect him at all. "Who's the foreman?" Tolya called out.

A large, squat, burly man wearing a wife-beater and construction helmet stepped forward. "That would be me. Afternoon officers."

"That would be detectives," Tolya said. "Detective Kurchenko." Tolya shook the foreman's hand. "And this is my partner, Detective Gonzalvez."

"Thanks for coming so quickly."

"We were around the corner." Tolya surveyed the demolition crew. They were dusty and sweating, some drinking from plastic water bottles, some smoking, almost all Latino. "You might want to send them home. This is a crime scene. They won't be working any more today."

The foreman lifted his eyebrows. "Wow, I don't have the authority to do that. I'm gonna have to call the office. Can you guys give me a minute?"

"Sure," replied Tolya.

"In the meantime," Pete said, "can we speak to the men who found the body?"

"Martinez, Abreu, come over here," the foreman called out. Two men walked hesitantly up the hill from some twenty feet away. Both in their early 20's, one was tall and thin, the other short and very muscular.

"*Ingles* or *español*?" Tolya asked.

The men looked at each other. "*Español*," they replied, nearly in unison.

Tolya smiled at Pete. "All yours."

Pete pulled the men aside. Tolya listened with one ear while monitoring the foreman's frenetic phone conversation with the other. He laughed to himself. He understood a few words of Pete's Spanish and the answers the construction guys gave him, but not one word of what the foreman said. Tolya couldn't even identify the language. Whoever the foreman was talking to was screaming back, his anger evident through the phone. Tolya's phone rang. "Yes, Captain." He could hear the same voice he heard through the foreman's phone in the background, only this time screaming in heavily accented English.

"I've got the owner on the other line," said the captain. He's freaking out about closing down. Says they're behind schedule. What's the story?"

"We don't know, yet." Tolya put his hand over his mouth and turned away, the foreman staring directly at him and clearly unhappy. "We're waiting for them to take us in. Pete's talking with the two guys who found the body."

"Okay. Just go in and call me when you're done. We're gonna have to close it down, but I'm not gonna tell the owner that till you call me back. I don't want any problems right now."

"Got it." Tolya clicked off. He turned to Pete. "What's the story?"

"They were in the first building, the one farthest down the hill, on the top floor, breaking down the walls with sledgehammers. When they hit the wall on the west side of the bedroom on the top floor, the plaster crumbled too easily. They pulled it down with their hands and in between the interior and exterior walls there was a body, still clothed, even has a hat on." Pete struggled to suppress a smile and lowered his voice. "They freaked out. Ran out of the building. They don't want to go back in."

Tolya smiled as well. "Superstitious?"

"Ya' think?"

Tolya turned to the foreman. "We gotta take a look."

The foreman waved at the two workers who found the body. They averted their eyes, attempting to ignore him. He shook his head and mumbled something in his language. "Follow me," he called to Tolya and Pete.

They circled around the crane into the site. "Watch your step here," the foreman said, pointing to the cracked steps that led to the front door of the old wood house. "It's a little wobbly."

"The two men who found the body, I'd like them to come with us," said Tolya.

"That ain't happening," the foreman said.

Tolya looked at Pete. "They're not going back in there, brother. They told me they're not coming back here for work either." Pete shook his head. "Don't force it."

The heat became even more stifling inside the old house, the windows having been painted shut for decades. Where the glass had broken—which was pretty much everywhere—there were sheets of plywood hammered over the frames. The place stank, a combination of garbage, and animal and human waste that had accumulated over decades. They covered their mouths and noses with their hands.

The foreman pointed a flashlight to the dilapidated stairs. "It's not as bad upstairs," he said. "We unsealed the windows up there, there's some ventilation."

Visibility increased as they approached the third floor. The foreman pointed left, to the back room. Tolya and Pete walked gingerly, the floorboards creaking. Inside the wall between two windows was a body sitting on a chair dressed in a suit with a hat perched on its head. It was an odd sight, something completely out of context; almost like something in a dream that makes the dreamer question the authenticity of the scene.

Calling the thing in the chair a body was giving it more credit than it deserved. It was more like a cross between a skeleton and a mummy. There was still some thin, cracking skin stretched across the bones. What was clear was that it had been there a long time.

Pete and Tolya pulled out the rubber gloves they always carried with them and slid them on with a snap. "Never seen anything like that before," Tolya said. "How long you think he's been in there?"

"Long time," said Pete, leaning in and examining the body more closely. "Look at the style of the suit, double-breasted with those wide lapels."

The suit hung on the skeleton like a clothing hanger with nothing to fill it out. There was a large, dark, bloodstain on the left side of the jacket, mid torso. "I can see why those guys were scared and didn't want to come back up here. That's really creepy."

Tolya unbuttoned the jacket and pulled it away from the skeleton gently so as not to disturb the fragile remains. Beneath the jacket, a white, sleeveless T-shirt, exactly like the wife-beater the foreman was wearing, hung from the bones. Tolya pointed to the large, dark stain on the T-shirt, mirroring the one on the jacket and the tear in its fabric. "Looks like that's where a bullet entered." The tear in the fabric corresponded to the location of the spleen. "The bleeding would have been very heavy." Tolya let the jacket slip gently back into place.

"Don't touch nothing else," Pete said. "That whole thing could just collapse."

"You're right. Let's get a CSU in here." He pulled out his cellphone and turned to the foreman. "I'm sorry my friend, but like I told you on the street, send your boys home. Work's done here for the next few days. This is a murder scene."

The foreman mumbled something in his language again.

"Where you from?" Tolya asked.

"Albania."

Chapter 2

Washington Heights, NYC
1 August 2008
2:00 p.m.

S halom Rothman peered out of the window from behind his desk on the third floor of his congregation's day school at the corner of 186th Street and Bennett Avenue. His window looked east and north over Broadway toward 187th Street. He could almost see the heat in the haze that hung in the air. Even with the air conditioner at full blast, it was still warm and humid in his office. As he mumbled the last phrase of his prayer after finishing lunch, he gazed at the three wood frame houses under demolition on the hill on 187th Street.

The neighborhood was changing. His community was shrinking. The young were moving away, mostly just across the George Washington Bridge to Teaneck, New Jersey, where they could have a small house with a yard. Many still sent their children back to his school for their education, and for the baby-sitting services their parents, who remained in the neighborhood, supplied in the afternoon. Before long, those who had left would open a school in their own community, and his world would shrink and dwindle even faster.

Shalom had considered this very same move many times for himself and his family. But Rachel would never leave her parents. After Baruch was diagnosed with autism, Shalom stopped trying to convince her to go. Now, there was no point. His responsibilities had grown. Rachel would be gone for at least five years. Baruch was settled into his school and finally making some progress, and he was the acting Rabbi. Rachel's tragedy had been too much for her father. He had stepped aside. His son had taken a position as a Rabbi in Florida. There was no one else. Shalom could never abandon the community that had adopted him.

He looked out again toward the three houses standing sentinel on the hill on 187th Street. They were an eyesore. He would be happy to see them go but would miss them at the same time. Perhaps *HaShem* was sending him a message. It was time to look forward, to forget the past, or at least store it away, forever.

He thought of Rachel. He missed her. He loved her. He always would, no matter what had happened. Those first few months without her had been very difficult, both because of Baruch and despite him. The boy was confused. He looked toward the door constantly, a sign to Shalom that in Baruch's non-verbal world he was asking a question, "Where is my mother?"

Taking care of Baruch was a full-time job in itself. Shalom had tried it alone at first. He hadn't wanted anyone around anyway, nor to discuss what had happened. Shalom preferred the solitude of his grief. He needed the space to make his own peace. Rachel's mother tried to help out, but every time she walked through the door she cried. And more likely than not the phone would ring shortly thereafter. It would be his father-in-law. He needed her to return home, immediately.

After a few months, Shalom realized he couldn't do it alone. He needed someone to help him with Baruch. The first two women, both from within the community, were a disaster. They didn't understand Baruch's condition and he didn't adjust to them at all. To the contrary, Shalom's cell phone rang within twenty minutes of his leaving every day. Even getting Baruch to school was more than they could handle.

Shalom needed someone who understood Baruch. He called María, the woman who had cared for Shalom's father before his death. She knew Baruch and understood his needs. Shalom hired her that day but made one thing very clear, he was not his father. She was never to bring any food into the house. He wouldn't trust her with kashruth.

About a month after María started, she asked Shalom if she could speak with him, freely and honestly.

"Of course," he responded.

"Rabbi Rothman," she pleaded in her quiet voice, her dark eyes averted. "I think Baruch need something more than me."

"Yes, of course, he needs his mother," replied Shalom, slipping on his suit jacket, "but that is clearly impossible."

"No, I was thinking something else."

Shalom stopped. He glanced at his watch, already late. He didn't really have time for this discussion on a subject he thought he had settled with the best possible solution. "What are you suggesting, María?"

"You remember Carlos?"

Shalom stiffened then shook his head. "I do, but no María, absolutely not."

"*Señor*, please listen to me."

"I can't have that boy here. Rachel would…" What could he say? The truth was the best lie in this case, "and after what happened I don't know that I can face him."

"You believe in the God, Rabbi?"

Shalom laughed. "María, please…"

"Rabbi, the God, he will help you. Don't feel the, how do you say, *verguenza*. I think you say embarrassed."

"That's the word, yes…"

"Baruch needs him. He understand Baruch and Baruch love him."

Shalom sighed, too harried to continue the discussion with María. "Let me think about it."

Shalom searched his soul that night and realized María was right. He asked her to contact Carlos. After meeting with him and apologizing more times than needed, Shalom offered him a job. Baruch was more moved than Shalom had ever seen him when Carlos arrived a few days later. He looked up from his ever-present books, smiled, ran up to Carlos and wrapped his arms around him, nearly knocking him over. Shalom was shocked. He could count on one hand the number of times he had seen Baruch touch another human being, particularly of his own volition. Tears streamed from Baruch's eyes. Shalom knew he had done the right thing.

Shalom looked at the clock. It was already 2:30. He packed his dirty plastics from lunch into his bag along with a volume of Talmud and took a few tissues from the box on his desk and slipped them into his pocket. It was just too hot for his jacket. He would carry it over his arm. He crossed the room to the air conditioner and turned it off, grabbed the bag and left, flicking off the light. As he opened the door to the hallway the heat and humidity hit him instantly. He took a deep breath. God willing this weather would change soon.

The walk to the school where Baruch spent his days was usually a pleasant one. Today though, Shalom took the bus. He saw it coming down the hill slowly from 181st Street and ran across Broadway against the light. He barely made it before the driver tried to pass the stop.

Baruch's school was located about a mile north at the base of Inwood in a building that had once been a synagogue. That congregation had died slowly. It hadn't had the unique character of his. Shalom's community had established itself, or perhaps the better term was re-established itself, in the years just before World War II, emigrating en-mass from two small towns in the Rhineland. They had transplanted their thousand-year-old way of life to the corner of 186th street and Bennett Avenue. They had their own customs, history, and story.

The other synagogues that had once populated the communities of upper Manhattan didn't have the same deep, all-encompassing roots. They were more reflective of the fast-changing character of the American Jewish experience—tradition was eschewed in favor of modernization. As people moved up the economic ladder, they moved away and communities dwindled, as his was doing now.

The pull of tradition and shared history paled in comparison to the siren song of America.

Shalom got off the bus just north of Nagle Avenue and walked the last two blocks to the school. He glanced at the YM/WHA a couple blocks up from Broadway. He'd met Rachel there. He longed to see her, to touch her. As he arrived at the building that housed the school—it would always be Congregation Beit Elohim to him—he wiped his forehead with the tissues he had taken from his office. The air was beyond still.

The sound of the children inside was clear and audible. As Shalom pushed the door open the cooled air caressed his face. He felt his pores close up on contact. He spotted Baruch at the far end of what had once been the main sanctuary. It was now a gym. Carlos was with him.

The city had installed a new wood floor when they converted the space to a school for special needs children. There were basketball hoops on backboards hung at six different spots along the walls suspended from the edge of the balcony that had once been the woman's section. He stopped for a moment to watch Baruch as he pointed the ball at the hoop and took his shot. Shalom smiled. Baruch made the shot more often than he missed. Carlos retrieved the ball and tossed it back to him. Baruch set up and shot again.

Carlos spotted Shalom and waved him over.

"How is he today?" Shalom asked.

"Excellent, better than ever."

"Is something different about today?" Shalom asked, finding Carlos' enthusiasm unexpected.

Carlos beamed. "What is that?" he called over to Baruch, pointing.

Baruch smiled. He held up the basketball. "Ball," he said.

Shalom walked over to Baruch and took the ball from his hands. He dropped it to the floor and pulled Baruch to him, his tears covering both their faces.

Chapter 3
Washington Heights, NYC
1 August 2008
4:30 p.m.

Seated at his desk, the Captain wiped the back of his neck with a wad of paper towel. "Damn, it's too hot." He stared at the photo of the body on Pete's iPhone. "Isn't that the damnedest thing? I've been a cop for nearly 30 years, I've never seen anything like that before."

"Us, neither," said Pete.

"And the hat? Can you imagine? The killer put the hat back on his head before he sealed up the wall," said Tolya.

"My uncles used to wear hats like that," said Pete.

"You got any missing uncles?" the Captain said, chuckling.

"A little creepy, if you ask me?" Tolya said. "How long before we have something back from the CSU?"

The Captain closed his eyes and leaned back into his chair, his stomach protruding over the desk. "Holy Jesus, Mary, and Joseph. We're investigating the death of a mummy. Let's not waste too much time on this, boys."

"We should take a more thorough look at the crime scene," Tolya thought out loud, walking with Pete down the long hallway toward the front of the station.

"Sure," said Pete. He laughed. "I guess that's the best place to start, at least till we get a report on King Tut. You're really into this crazy thing, aren't you, brother-man?"

"You know it. I always wanted to work a cold case. You wanna meet tomorrow morning at nine?"

Pete hesitated a moment. He didn't really want to waste time or energy on this case, especially on a weekend. He doubted there could be any resolution, but he would do it for Tolya, humor him, more for the sake of their friend-ship, than for the sake of justice for the unknown victim. "Okay, but let's work out first?" He had planned on meet-ing Tolya at the gym anyway, and this was a good way to get him up early. "Like seven?"

"Sure," Tolya replied, "Before it gets too hot."

"Don't forget your packages, Tol." Pete pointed to the two shopping bags on the floor filled with the plantains and yuca they had picked up after finding the dead man in the wall of the house on west 187th street. "You don't want to disappoint Karin."

This time Tolya took a swipe at Pete. "Jealous?"

"Seriously? You know how much yuca and platanos I've eaten in my life? I'm pushing Glynnis to cook Amer-ican." Pete opened the door and held it for Tolya. The heat was evident, immediately.

"Pete," Tolya said as they exited the building by the back door into the parking lot. "When do you think that suit was from? Looks like what the old communists would wear back in the Soviet Union when I was kid, but they were always twenty years behind in styles."

Pete thought for a moment. "If the guy was rich and American, I'd say the suit was from the 50's. But, if he was a poor immigrant like you and me, he could be wearing that suit ten years later."

Tolya felt a chill despite the heat as he pictured the body disappearing behind a fresh layer of plaster.

Pete turned right out of the precinct building. He waved at Tolya. "Enjoy the platanos." Tolya waved back. He took the slight incline on Broadway slowly. This heat was a little too much, even for him, hotter than it ever was in Santo Domingo.

The street was filled with people. Mothers and grand-mothers mostly with their children, the older ones a few feet ahead, the younger ones held by their hands, the strollers, more often than not occupied by an infant.

He thought of his own kids. He loved kids, especially babies. It was the thing most people didn't know about him. Under the tough guy exterior, he was a soft touch— but not just for his own kids, for pretty much all kids. Each kid was like a new start. Each one had that chance to be something unique. And besides, as the youngest he never had the opportunity to be the older brother, except for Chicho maybe, but Chicho was only eleven months younger than Pete. His cousins and nieces and nephews had given him that chance. And his own children after that, because he knew that to be a good father you needed to know when to be a parent and when to be a brother.

Pete crossed 181ˢᵗ street. The produce cart on the south corner was crowded with old ladies squeezing the fruit and the vegetables. "*Permiso*," he said to a tiny *abuela* in front of him. She moved to her left. "*No, no, disculpame*" he said touching her forearm gently. He pointed to the avocados. "*Por favor abuela, escojame uno.*"

Her smile lit up her face, the lines around her mouth and eyes, and the caramel color of her skin reminding him of his own mother. He missed her. He had missed too many years with her when she had left him on the island and came to New York before she was able to bring him. That was the reason he stayed in the apartment, her apartment. Somehow, he felt closer to her there, even after all these years since her death.

"*Por supesto, mijo*," the old woman said as she set about gently squeezing and pressing the large, bright-green fruit that Dominicans serve with virtually everything.

Pete felt an arm slip around his neck. He willed himself not to panic, grabbed for his gun, turned, then released his finger from the trigger. "*Coño*," he shouted, angry and laughing at the same time. "Don't ever do that! I could have killed you." He grabbed for his assailant and pulled him close, hugging him tightly. "Roberto, oh my god. How are you?"

"Good *tío*. And you?"

Pete pushed Roberto back to look at him, his hands still on his shoulders. "Damn, you're bigger than me. When did you get back?"

"About a month ago."

Pete dropped his hands from Roberto's shoulders, and took a step back. "And you haven't called?"

Roberto eyes dropped to the sidewalk. 'I'm sorry, *tío*. I wasn't ready to see anybody."

Pete moved closer. He brought his head near to Roberto's and whispered. "Was it that bad?"

Roberto nodded.

"I understand. You know if you need to talk..."

Roberto looked at him. "I know, *tío*. Just give me a little time."

The old woman touched Pete's elbow. "*Aqui, mijo*," she said, handing him an avocado.

"*Gracias, abuela*," Pete said. "You take what time you need. But right now, you're coming home with me to see Glynnis and the kids. And to have some dinner."

Roberto smiled. "Okay, but no questions about Afghanistan."

୧୬୧

Tolya stood in the doorway of Max's room watching Karin as she put him into his crib. She stood over the bed and caressed Max's cheek. Tolya loved to watch her. Her beauty as a mother intoxicated him even more than her beauty alone before Max came along. Fifteen months after becoming a father, his reticence about fatherhood and what it would do to his relationship with Karin had become incomprehensible to him.

Karin walked toward him, closing the door to Max's room half-way. He put his arms around her waist. She caressed his cheek as she had Max's and kissed him gently on the lips. "I love you," she said.

"I love you, too."

She took his hand and led him back down the hallway to the living room. They sat down on the black leather couch, Karin in the corner, stretching out and leaning back into the soft pillows. Tolya placed his hand on her belly. He could feel the baby move. "He's got strong legs."

"Yes, another soccer player." Karin placed her hand on Tolya's. He leaned and lowered his lips to hers, kissing her deeply. She smiled, caressing his cheek again propping herself on her elbow. "I want you more than ever Tolya Kurchenko, but not tonight. I'm dead tired. You know how these last three months go. Would you help me up so I can get this body into bed?"

Tolya chuckled. He offered her his hand. She grabbed him by the forearm and leveraged herself up off the couch. "Should I come to bed with you?"

"Only if you're ready to go to sleep," Karin replied. "I'm sorry, but once I lay down the exhaustion overtakes me."

He put his arms around her again and kissed her on the forehead. "That's okay. I understand. I'm not ready for bed. I'm gonna do a little research."

"New case?"

"Perhaps. I'll tell you about it in the morning."

Karin kissed him on the cheek and walked slowly up the two steps from the living room to the hallway. "Good night," she called back softly as she disappeared down the hall that led to the bedrooms.

Tolya sat down at his desk and turned on the new Apple computer he had purchased a few weeks earlier. He clicked on Safari and brought up a browser page then typed the address of the buildings on 187th street into the search box. In a nano-second Google loaded. The top hit was an article from a blog called The Uptown Collective. Tolya clicked on it. It was an editorial from the blogger, Led Black, on the accelerating gentrification of the neighborhood. The article provided Tolya with some useful basic information; the years the original buildings were built, the history of their useful life beginning as middle-class private homes and ending as tiny, cut-up apartments for the poor, and now to their demolition to make way for "luxury housing," for the neighborhood's current upswing.

Two things on the blog post impressed Tolya, the old black and white photo that showed the original stand of six houses, and the depth of knowledge this guy had about both the houses and the neighborhood.

Chapter 4

Tolya pushed open the wooden gate to the deserted construction site on West 187th Street. He and Pete hung their gym bags on the broken limb of a dead tree in front of the old house. The graying, tortured stump would be bull-dozed away with the rest of the debris when the demolition was complete. Pete took the small flashlight from his pocket and pressed against the front door. "Let's go."

They walked carefully up the stairs. The room was exactly as they had left it, minus the body. The CSU had come and gone. The hole in the wall appeared a little strange without the mummy perched inside. Tolya paced slowly, pantherlike, back and forth, across the small room.

"What exactly are we looking for, Tol? You think the CSU missed something?"

"I'm not sure brother, I just wanted a second look. I want to feel what might have happened."

Pete chuckled to himself. "Okay, see if you get any vibes." He was used to this after so many years partnered with Tolya. He crouched in the corner opposite the windows.

Tolya continued walking silently around the room, imagining what it might be like filled with furniture. The bed would have been opposite the windows, but there was an old radiator where he expected the bed to sit. No. He realized, the body had been in the wall since the 60's or earlier, and at that time there likely wasn't any air-conditioning. The bed would have been under the windows to catch the breeze. There might have been a dresser, or more likely a large armoire on the opposite wall, as the room didn't have a closet. The floorboards creaked as he walked back and forth.

"Well, you feeling anything yet?" Pete asked. He wiped his forehead with the back of his forearm then looked at his watch. "Damn it's hot in here, and it's only 9:45."

Tolya stopped pacing. "I don't think he was killed in this room."

Pete was caught a little off guard, though he shouldn't have been. They had been partners for more than ten years, yet he was still amazed and a little freaked out by Tolya's ability to imagine the crime almost frame by frame in his mind. "Why?"

"The room is too small. He waved his arm toward the northwest corner of the space. "If you put a bed here to catch the breeze, and you had a big free-standing closet and maybe a dresser where you're sitting, you would have to get too close to the victim. The fabric on the wife beater would show more damage. The hole was too clean. There had to be more distance between the shooter and the victim than there could have been in this room."

Pete encouraged Tolya, a proven method in this situation. "Okay, then where do you think he was killed?"

Tolya took Pete's flashlight from beside the doorway and ran down the stairs. Pete followed despite the bad smell still lingering on the lower floors. Tolya looked around the second-floor apartment and continued down to the first floor. "When do you think they reconfigured the place into apartments?" he shouted.

Pete looked around at the skeleton of the second floor from the landing. The kitchen was to the rear. The kitchen on the third floor was in the front. "Not at one time. Nothing is uniform." He took the steps down to the first floor two at a time. "The kitchens are wherever there are plumbing lines," Pete said, "and not on the same plumbing line, which means originally there were plenty of bathrooms."

Tolya searched around the floor with the flashlight. He spotted a crowbar in the corner of the room and grabbed it. He wedged it in at the bottom of the large plywood sheet that covered the window and pulled. The board gave way easily, the bright August morning light and humid air fresher than what was locked in the room flooding in from outside. "How do you think this was laid out before it was cut up?"

Pete walked to the wall that separated the room where they were standing from the one behind it and tapped. It was hollow, not the plaster and lathe walls that delineated rooms in buildings of this vintage. "This wall was put in later to cut the space in half. This was probably a big parlor, originally. The kitchen would have been at the back."

Tolya took several steps into the hallway, which ran the length of the floor. In fact, behind the front room was another room, and beyond that a kitchen. "Could you grab that crowbar and come in here, please," he called out.

Pete pried the wood planks off the window in the middle room. The light revealed details the darkness had obscured. The walls, dirty, dusty, and faded, were covered from the floor to chest height with wood wainscoting. The pattern of the wainscoting changed along the wall. He tapped on it. "Hear that shallow sound?" he said. "Just like in the other room. This piece of wall was also added later." He ran his fingers along the ridge at the top of the molding. Despite the years of grime and layers of paint he could detect where a new piece of molding was placed to match the original. It was just slightly out of line. "There was an opening here."

Tolya knelt in front of the wall near the corner and ran his hands over the wainscoting with closed eyes. Decades of carpentry and DIY home repairs came in handy. He let his fingers search for evidence that not even years of neglect and cosmetic fixes could make disappear. He found something about two feet from the corner at waist level. There were three small holes in the wood panel which had been patched with wood plugs and painted over. They were raised just enough from the original wood panel to be evident to the touch. "Look at this," he said,

"What?"

Tolya took Pete's hand. "Close your eyes." He put Pete's fingertips on the wood and ran them over the plugs. "You feel it?"

Pete laughed. "Yeah, I do, plugs, about the size of a bullet hole. Maybe King Tut was shot here." He opened his eyes and looked at Tolya, a big grin on his face. "Proud of yourself, Detective?"

"Sure am."

Chapter 5
Washington Heights, NYC
3 August 2008
10:30 a.m.

Tolya pushed open the exterior door to the foyer of 222 Wadsworth Ave and pressed the buzzer for apartment 6A. The hallway walls were painted a stale shade of green, made even more institutional by the insufficient lighting. Thankfully, there was an elevator. He took it to the sixth floor.

The apartment doors told a story. They were alternately old, chipped and ill-fitting in their frames, or new, freshly painted, and tight in their casings. He paused a moment and counted the doors then noted where they appeared along the walls, three old doors, four new doors, the new ones' closer together than they should have been. Tolya knew immediately, the landlord cut up the old units as they became vacant. This building was changing, as was the neighborhood.

Tolya knocked on one of the old doors. "Yes, coming," he heard from inside. A moment later a man of about 5'8" in his early 40's, his skin the color of coffee with cream, dressed in jeans and a T-shirt that read "Spread the Uptown

Love" stood before him, a welcoming grin on his face, his hand extended. "I'm, Led Black," he said.

"Nice to meet you, Tolya Kurchenko."

"Please, come in."

Tolya followed Led down the long hallway toward the living room at its end. He passed several bedrooms and then a large kitchen on the right. The living room was filled with couches and club chairs. The walls were painted a cheerful yellow, the color heightened by the sunlight that streamed through the lace curtains covering the windows. Family photographs and framed paintings depicting various pastoral Caribbean scenes covered the walls.

"Would you like something to drink? Coffee?"

"Sure," Tolya replied, sitting down on one of the couches.

"How do you take it?"

"*Con leche, sin azucar*," Toyla replied.

Led's face lit up. "You speak Spanish?"

Tolya laughed. "That's pretty much the extent of it. My wife is Dominican."

"*Familia! Mama*," he called down the hallway, "*Por favor, dos café con leche!*"

A short woman in her 60's appeared. She smiled and nodded. "*Sí, por supuesto, mijo.*"

"This is my mother, Esmeralda Fuentes. *Mama esta es el* Detective Kurchenko."

"*Encantado*," Tolya said. Esmeralda moved to the kitchen in full view from the living room, and bowed her head slightly, her son's smile an exact copy of hers.

"This is my mother's apartment," Led said, sitting down at the Formica table. "I grew up here."

"Where do you live now?"

"Jersey, but we're trying to move back. It's tough with three kids. Apartments are out of sight."

Led's mother brought the coffees. She placed them on the table, along with a plate of small pastries. "I made them, please try," she said, then retreated back to the kitchen.

Tolya took one and bite into it. The buttery, crusty pastry was filled with guava jelly, sweet and tangy.

"So, Detective, how can I help you?"

"I saw your story online about the old houses on 187th street and I wanted to find out more about the buildings."

Led leaned forward, his elbows on the table. "Sure. May I ask, what do you want to know, and why?

Tolya hesitated. "Off the record. It can't get into your blog."

"No problem," replied Led.

"We found a dead body entombed in the wall of one of the houses during demolition a couple of days ago." Watching Led's face for a reaction, Tolya was expecting surprise, but instead, got something more akin to confirmation.

"Wow," Led chuckled. "That makes a lot of sense."

Tolya was caught off guard. "How so?"

"When we were kids, we used to say that house was haunted."

Tolya smiled. "Really? Tell me more, please."

Led took a sip of his coffee and one of his mother's pastries. "There was a story that someone was murdered in the house, but the body was never found."

"If there was no body, what started the rumor?"

"The place was a boarding house back then. One of the boarders disappeared. It became, you know, an urban legend."

Tolya sipped the last of what was in his cup. "Your mother makes great coffee."

"Thanks. Would you like another?"

"No, that's fine. Why did they suspect that the guy was murdered? Maybe he just left? Boarders are transient, they tend to do that."

"He had a girlfriend and a few friends. They reported him missing. Some neighbors in the building next door claimed to hear some fighting and gunshots the night before he disappeared. Shortly after that, they closed, and the building was reconfigured into apartments. Invariably, after a tenant or their kids learned of the story, they claimed to be hearing things at night."

Tolya laughed. "How do you know this?"

Led smiled. "I'm the mayor of Washington Heights. I've made a life's work of knowing everything there is to know about this neighborhood."

"When did this happen?"

"1966."

It was still early when Pete arrived at the precinct. Glynnis wouldn't give him too much trouble about working on his day off if he got back by 1:00. Besides, he had promised Tolya he would do some snooping around online about King Tut.

"Good morning, Detective," said the duty officer as he signed in. He flashed his most seductive smile at her before he headed down the hall. Though he had learned his lesson about too much overt flirting, he just couldn't help himself sometimes. Besides, it kept him in practice.

"Detective," a voice boomed out before he passed the captain's office. The duty officer must have buzzed alerting him Pete was here.

"Yes, sir," Pete replied, standing in the hallway in front of the Captain's door.

"Glad to see you're here on a Sunday." The Captain smiled and stared him down good naturedly. "Where's your partner?'

Pete shook his head. "Not sure, Captain."

The Captain cleared his throat. "You working that mummy?"

"Yes Captain, you said…"

The Captain rolled his eyes. "Try to wrap that up as quick as possible. I sense your partner is just a little too fascinated by this case."

"Will do."

Pete continued down the hall to the office he shared with Tolya. It was comfortably warm. If Tolya were here, he would complain it was too warm. He flicked on the light, sat down at his desk, turned on his computer. After a moment, the screen lit up and he signed in. He typed the address of the wood frame house, 669 West 187th Street, into the google search bar along with the words, newspaper articles.

Several articles came up, mostly to do with the neighborhood controversy surrounding the construction of the new building. Tolya had already briefed him on them, so he skipped them. Buried on the next search page was an article from the New York Post, dated October 29, 1985. It was about haunted houses in the five boroughs. 669 West 187th Street was detailed last. The article was decidedly tongue in cheek, as would be expected for something published two days before Halloween. It did though reveal the name of the man who had disappeared. He was reportedly a Cuban refugee named Fernando Vargas. Miriam Rivera, who claimed to be his girlfriend, reported his disappearance. Since his clothes and other belongings were gone, the police simply assumed he had skipped out on his rent. The article didn't mention the boarding house operator by name.

Pete brought up another browser page and typed Fernando Vargas into the search bar. Numerous photos of various men named Fernando Vargas came up. He added the building's address and Miriam Rivera to the search, narrowing the results dramatically. There at the top of the list was an article from the New York Post archive. He clicked on it, then typed in the precinct password into the subscription bar, and in another nano-second there was an interview of Miriam Rivera from a 1990 article on unsolved disappearances. The New York Post clearly loved this story. They wouldn't let it die.

This time Rivera's picture was included in the story. She was dressed in a style that indicated she was delighted to have her fifteen minutes in the spotlight. She insisted there was no way Vargas had run off. They were in love and planned to be married. Except here she referred to him as an immigrant from the Dominican Republic. The article gave her address as 105 Wadsworth Avenue, literally around the corner from the house on 187th Street.

Pete entered her name and address and the word "phone" into another search bar and clicked enter. There she was. It was 18 years later, but she was still at the same address. He laughed to himself. People who paid low rents under rent stabilization or rent control for an apartment with multiple bedrooms lived to be very old and they didn't move, the bane of a landlord's existence. Good for her. He jotted down the number then sent a request to the archives for a search of the cold case files for Fernando Vargas.

Chapter 6
Washington Heights, NYC
4 August 2008
9:30 a.m.

Ms. Rivera," Tolya said, "thanks for seeing us on such short notice."

"You're welcome, Officers."

Tolya hesitated a moment. He caught Pete's look and stopped himself.

"We're detectives, *señora*," Pete said, a grin on his face.

"Oh, sorry," said Rivera, crossing her legs. She corrected her posture sitting on the edge of the green velvet club chair, the fabric of her black skirt creeping above her knees as she did so. Rivera picked up a tiny demitasse cup and moved it to her lips, sipping at her espresso. When she returned the cup to its saucer, bright red lipstick lined its edge.

"That's all right," Tolya said. He stifled a grin but kept his eyes on Rivera. He knew if he looked at Pete, they would both likely begin to laugh. Rivera was clearly relishing her next fifteen minutes of fame. She was dressed for an evening of club hopping circa 1975 at 9:30 on a Monday morning. "Do you mind answering some questions about the disappearance of Fernando Vargas."

Rivera smiled and took another sip of her coffee. "*Ay, que triste*, you know detective he was the great love of my life."

"Yes, you've said that," Tolya replied. He glanced at Pete who had settled back into the corner of the couch covered in the same plush green velvet as the chair. Pete lifted one corner of his mouth into a half grin. "*Señora*," he said, "if you prefer, we can interview you in Spanish."

"No, Detective. I able to speak English very well."

"Okay then," said Tolya, "let's get started. Could you tell us again what happened when Vargas disappeared?"

Rivera placed both of her hands on her left knee, one atop of the other, and lifted her chin, her demeanor theatrical. "Like I always say, he was murder."

"But how do you know this?" said Tolya, leaning in toward Rivera.

Rivera took a deep breath, raising her chin even higher. "He would never leave me."

"Perhaps we should try this another way, *señora*," said Pete, his large frame now hovering over the glass coffee table. "We know what you said in the past. And we believe you. Did Vargas have any enemies?"

Rivera shook her head. "No, no, that I know. Everybody he know like him very much, but you know he was a very quiet person. Very private."

"Did he have any friends? Tolya asked. "Or enemies?"

Rivera pursed her lips and shook her head from side to side. "No. He was very quiet. He went to work every day and he came home, and he saw me."

"Two other people reported him missing as well. Did you know them?"

"Detective, was a long time ago, I don't remember. Maybe was someone from his work."

"Where did he work?"

"In a Cuban restaurant, downtown. He works in the kitchen."

"Do you remember the name of the restaurant?"

Rivera nodded. "*Sí,* Havana Estrella, but is close for a long time. It was on the corner of 51st Street and Eight Avenue. They build a big building there."

"Ms. Rivera," Tolya continued, "you said in an interview with the New York Post back in 1990 that Mr. Vargas was Dominican, but earlier reports say he was Cuban. Was he Dominican or Cuban?"

Rivera reached for a cigarette. "Do you mind?"

"No, go right ahead," Tolya replied, despite how much he detested tobacco smoke. It was her apartment. Also, he wanted her to open up. If smoking would help, he would choke his way through it.

Rivera took the cigarette from a pack of Virginia Slims on the coffee table and placed it between her lips. She looked at Pete and smiled. Pete picked up the cheap, red, plastic lighter from the coffee table and lit her cigarette. "*Gracias, mi amor,*" Rivera purred, taking a long drag and letting it out slowly. Despite himself, Tolya coughed. "Ms. Rivera, was he Dominican or Cuban?"

"He was Dominican. But the newspaper at the time they say Cuban, because he work at a Cuban restaurant so…" She smiled at Pete. "*Sabes que los blanquitos no conocen las diferencias entre los latinos.*"

Tolya looked at Pete.

"She said, to white people we're all the same."

Rivera's cheeks, the color of toffee, blushed, visible even under her heavy makeup. "Sorry." She crushed her cigarette into the ceramic ashtray on the small, wood end table next to the club chair.

"That's okay," Tolya said. "No offense taken. As a matter of fact, I believe you're right. Where did you meet Fernando Vargas?"

Rivera sat back in the chair. She smiled. "At a night club there used to be on 175th street. It was call Las Palmas. It was a dance club. He were a very good dancer."

"Was he living at the rooming house around the corner when you met?"

"No. He were living downtown in the west 50's, near the restaurant. He would come to the club to meet other Dominican people. That's where he met the guy from the rooming house."

"Another boarder?" Pete asked.

"No, the guys who owned the house."

"Guy or guys? There was more than one?"

"*Sí*, two guys. He met them at the club. One night we were listening to the music having a drink. It was a merengue band from Santo Domingo, that's why he wanted to go there that night. Nando, he go to the men's room and he told me this man invite us to his table. Nando say the man remember him from Santo Domingo."

"What did Vargas say?"

"He say he didn't remember him, but they bought some drinks and they start talking to each other and they become friendly."

"When did he move into the rooming house?"

Rivera hesitated a moment. "You know I has to think about this a little bit." Rivera closed her eyes and counted on her left hand using the fingers of her right. After a long moment she opened them and smiled. "I remember now. It was about a month later. We was walking on the street here and they see us on the street and come over. I remember they say to him he should move into their rooming house; they would make a good price for him."

"And how long was this before he disappeared?"

"It was maybe two months."

"Were there other people living there?"

Rivera smiled. "I don't remember, was long ago. I remember the two men they own the building." She smiled and took another cigarette from the pack, this time lighting it herself. "I helping you, detectives?"

"*Sí*," Pete said.

"I so happy. Finally, somebody want to solve the mystery of what happened to my Nando."

"Ms. Rivera…"

"Please, detective, call me Miriam,"

"Okay, Miriam," said Tolya, "Please try to remember. Were there any other boarders?"

Rivera took a drag on the cigarette. After she exhaled, she slid her upper lip under her bottom teeth, holding the cigarette up with her right hand, her elbow resting on the arm of the chair. She was pensive for a moment then flicked the growing ash off the cigarette into the dusty, nearly full, ashtray. "When he move in, I think yes. There were three rooms, on the top floor and three rooms on the second floor. One of the owners, he live in two of the rooms on the second floor and one they rent out, so four people renting. When Nando move in there were two rooms he could pick from. Yes, I remember now. There was two other people, then they move out."

"The owner didn't get new tenants?"

"No."

"Do you remember the owners' names?"

"Let me see, the one guy he was, Henrique. The other I don't remember."

Tolya glanced at Pete then slid the pad he was taking notes on back into the accordion folder he had brought it in. "*Gracias, señora*, no," Tolya said, "unless my partner has something he'd like to ask you."

"I think that's all for now," said Pete.

"My pleasure," Rivera said, leaning back in the chair and taking one last drag off the nearly spent cigarette.

ເ∕ວເ∕ວ

A medium-sized, gray, cardboard box, dusty and moldy smelling, was waiting for them when they returned. Pete lifted it off the floor and planted it on his desk, removing the top. "Not much here," he said, peering inside.

"Nope," Tolya replied, peering into the murky carton. He took out the case file yellowed from age and opened it. The paper inside was brown around the edges and crumbled easily. "Better be careful with this," he said, mostly for himself, placing the case file on his side of the double desk then slipping on a pair of latex gloves. "Here," he said, handing a pair to Pete as well.

Tolya began reciting the first page of the report. The cursive handwriting was clear and easily read, surprising for a cop's penmanship.

"One Fernando Vargas was reported missing by his girlfriend, Miriam Rivera, on July 6, 1966. Officer Mack O'Conner and myself have inspected his residence. The premises is a unit in a rooming house located at 669 West 187th Street. The room formerly occupied by said Fernando Vargas is located on the third (top) floor at the rear of the house. The missing person appears to have taken all his possessions with him and left in the middle of the night on July 4,1966.

"We interviewed one owner of the rooming house, a Mr. Ernest Eisen, who operates the business with a partner. He reported that they last saw Mr. Vargas in the shared living room of the rooming house at about 9 p.m., July 4, 1966 at which time they left the premises to attend a party a few blocks away. They noted that the next morning, when they attempted entrance to Mr. Vargas' room to clean it, they found him, and his possessions gone. They stated that he owed them two months' rent and assumed he had run out in the middle of the night. He was at this time, the only boarder in the rooming house.

"It is the considered opinion of this officer after examination and investigation of the circumstances that in fact Vargas simply left with the intent of avoiding payment of his back rent, a ploy commonly used by people of his background. There is no indication of foul play.

Officer Thomas Anderson
July 8, 1966"

Tolya flipped the rest of the pages in the folder gingerly. "These are the records of the interviews they conducted," he said to Pete, lifting the corners of the pages carefully— Rivera, some guy named Roberto Garcia and another named Ramfis Abreu. I guess we can read them through later. Is there anything else in the box?"

Pete withdrew another folder. "These," he said, thumbing through a series of old black and white photos.

Tolya looked them over as well. The first was marked on the back with the name of the victim. He was tall, thin and wore a pencil-line mustache. His dark hair was brushed back and slicked down in the style of the time. A cigarette hung from his mouth. In a second photo, he was standing with two men. "These guys look familiar," Tolya said.

Pete lifted his mouth into a half smile. "C'mon Tol. That picture is older than you. And how would you know those guys, anyway? You didn't come to this country till twelve years later."

"I've seen them before." Tolya smiled and pointed at the two figures in the photo. "Look harder, you know them."

Pete took back the picture and stared at it. "You're right, they do look a little familiar."

Tolya sat down in front of his computer. He had a good idea who the men in the photo were, but he wanted additional proof, and liked the idea of playing with Pete's head just a little bit, dragging out the reveal of the information he was pretty sure he would confirm momentarily. He clicked on the icon for Lexis Nexis. The homepage loaded, he entered the precinct password and waited for the search page to appear. He typed in the address for the building on 187th street and the phrase, title records. The ownership history of the property appeared before him. Tolya read down the list of transfers slowly, going back through the years to 1966. When he found the transfer he was looking for, he pointed out the names of the sellers.

"*Coño*," Pete said. "That's crazy."

Chapter 7

Washington Heights, NYC
4 August 2008
12:30 p.m.

S halom was hunched over the desk reviewing the applications for admission to the kindergarten class for the coming year. He wouldn't have many decisions to make in terms of selecting students. For the very first time since he began teaching at the school some fifteen years earlier, there were more seats in the classroom than there were applicants. It was only a matter of time, a few years, before the school would be in serious trouble. He knew he had to find a way to grow the community. He also knew its insular nature would make that improbable, if not all together impossible. Faigl's voice broke his concentration.

"Yes?"

"Sorry to disturb you, Rabbi?"

"Come in," he replied. "You're not disturbing me."

A tall, thin, nervous, young woman in a long, brown skirt and long-sleeved, white top entered. Her head was covered with a brown snood, a wisp of reddish hair astray around her left ear. Shalom gestured to her to tuck it in.

"Sorry," she said as she pushed the thin hairs back under their cloth covering. "There are two men here. They would like to see you." She averted her gaze then continued. "Policemen."

Shalom rose from the desk. Faigl handed him their cards. Shalom nodded. "Show them in, please."

Faigl hurried from the room. Shalom took his coat from behind his chair and slipped it on, despite the fact that the room was warm notwithstanding the ever-humming air conditioner. "Good morning, detectives," Shalom said. "To what do I owe this honor?"

"May we sit?" Tolya said smiling. "It's been a while."

"Of course," Shalom said, gesturing to the chairs opposite his desk then shaking their hands. "I trust both of you are well?"

Tolya sat in the chair to the right. A memory ran through his mind of that very first time he sat in this room some thirty years earlier. The Rabbi was different, but the feel was the same. And the memory chilled him, even in this heat. "We are well," Tolya replied, "and you?"

Shalom took a breath and hesitated a moment. "Well enough, considering the circumstances."

"And your wife?" Tolya asked.

Shalom considered his response before answering. He thought the question inappropriate. There was no point to being confrontational though. He had accepted what had happened to Rachel, and Kurchenko's and Gonzalvez's parts in it.

"Also, well enough," Shalom replied. An awkward silence further cluttered the already claustrophobic space.

Shalom looked from Tolya to Pete and back again. "How can I help you?"

Pete took an envelope from his rear pocket and opened it withdrawing a single piece of paper. He handed it to Shalom. "Look at the name at the bottom of this, please."

Shalom stared at the print-out of the title history for the property at 669 West 187th Street. He felt his breakfast creep up into his throat. There at the bottom was his father's name. "And what is it you would like me to know about this?"

Tolya grinned and leaned a bit forward in the chair. It was as hard and uncomfortable as he remembered it from his first and subsequent visits. "Did you know that your father owned the building up there on 187th?" He pointed through the window at the construction site.

"Yes, of course I knew that. He ran a rooming house there for some ten or twelve years, when I was a boy. That was their business in Europe you know, my parents, they owned a small hotel. Though I expect you knew that already, as you're quite familiar with my father's life. Perhaps, more so than I."

Tolya sat back in the chair, pausing for the shortest of moments. He wanted to make Shalom a little anxious. Then he grinned, locking his eyes on Shalom's, his smile more aggressive than genuine. "I do recall something to that effect. We have a question for you. Who is Ernest Eisen?"

Shalom gazed out the window to the buildings on West 187th. He felt suspended in time. He had lived too much of his life within these small streets and felt as if they were beginning to close in on him. Beyond the windows, there was haze in the air. The crane on 187th Street was silent. No work had gone on there for a few days. He had wondered why. Now he knew something was amiss. "You know him," Shalom snapped. "Eisen, Hierron, they have the same basic meaning, in Yiddish and in Spanish, iron."

"Henrique Hierron?" Pete said.

"Yes, they are one and the same."

"I expected so," said Tolya.

Shalom took a breath. He wasn't going to let Kurchenko or his partner intimidate him. "What are you looking into here?" he asked.

"May I speak off the record?"

"Of course." Shalom forced a smile. "Consider it privileged, clergy-congregant confidentiality."

Tolya smiled back, the same insincere smirk he had offered a few moments earlier. "We found a body in the building." He watched Shalom's face for a reaction, but none was forthcoming.

"I can't imagine what that would have to do with either my father or Erno," Shalom said. "They sold the property when I was a kid, some forty years ago, and neither of them could have committed a fresh murder. My father is dead and Erno is in a wheelchair and close to 100 years old."

"The body wasn't fresh," said Pete. "In fact, it's been hidden for some time. The demolition crews found it a few days ago."

"No wonder I haven't seen any work going on," said Shalom, fidgeting with the papers on his desk.

"Exactly. There have been rumors of a murder in the property that date from the time when your father and Erno

owned it. How old were you when the building was sold?"
Tolya asked.

Shalom looked at the date on the transfer record and
chuckled. "Twelve, a little past twelve. You mean those
stories about it being haunted?"

"Perhaps they're not stories. Do you recall why they
sold the property?"

"Yes," Shalom replied. "The business was dying. No
pun intended. They had catered to refugees like themselves
for many years. The number of Jewish survivors from the
war seeking a room, as well as the number of young Jewish
people coming into the neighborhood had declined significantly by the early 1960's. They began renting to people
from Puerto Rico, Cuba, the Dominican Republic, since
they spoke Spanish. These tenants often disappeared in the
middle of the night without paying. Often rooms would be
empty for long stretches. My father was offered a job as
general manager of a hotel in midtown, so they sold the
building and closed down the business. That money paid
for my college education."

Tolya nodded his head slightly, his index fingers together, touching his lips. "Interesting, is there anything
else you remember about the place? Any of the boarders?"

Shalom gazed out the window again. There was nothing
about the building, or the business, or the phantoms that
inhabited it, that he cared to remember. "It was a long time
ago. I didn't spend much time there. If you want to know
more, you need to speak with Erno. You know where to
find him," Shalom said, turning his eyes back to the list on
his desk.

"Thanks for your time," Tolya said, both he and Pete getting up.

Shalom raised his head. "If there is anything else, let me know." He didn't offer his hand in farewell, as he normally would. He wanted to be done with these two.

"Thanks, we will," Tolya replied.

Shalom sat back down as the door clicked shut. He took two tissues from the box on his desk and patted his forehead. His breakfast creeped up into his throat again, this time a little higher. Shalom breathed deeply to calm himself. He still had conflicted feelings about his father and expected he would for the rest of his life. Since his father's death, Shalom had put their conflicts out of his mind. The demolition on 187th had brought it back, and this visit from Kurchenko and his partner only made it worse.

Shalom thought of Rachel. Thinking of her always calmed him. He closed his eyes and pictured her face, serene and happy. He recalled the day they met. He was home from Brandeis for spring break. He had gone to the YM/WHA on Nagle Avenue to meet a friend from high school and to play some basketball. After changing back into street clothes, they had gone into the cafeteria to have a snack. His friend had recently started keeping kosher. The cafeteria at the "Y" was strictly kosher, and therefore easier for Morty to navigate than the tiny Greek coffee shops that populated the neighborhood at that time. Shalom closed his eyes. He could see Rachel as clearly as he did that day.

Washington Heights, NY
March 1975

"What are you staring at?" Morty asked him.

Stephen felt himself blush. He nodded to his right. "She's beautiful."

Morty smiled. "Very. Do you know who she is?"

Stephen shook his head.

"The daughter of Rabbi Schoenweiss, from the synagogue across from your building."

Stephen remained silent. He sipped at his coffee and took a bite of the cheese Danish he'd bought at the counter. He laughed to himself. Despite his desire to rid himself of his parents' Hungarian behaviors, he couldn't drink coffee without pastry and always preferred cheese Danish to anything else."

"Don't waste your time, Steph," Morty said. "She won't speak to a man, let alone one who isn't *frum*."

"I imagine you're right about that." He continued to watch her as she got up from the table, zipped and buttoned the jackets of the children she was tending, and led them out of the cafeteria.

Stephen popped the last of the Danish into his mouth. "So, how is this kosher thing going?" he asked Morty.

"Pretty good, most of the time. Sometimes I get a craving for a cheeseburger or Chinese food. But it's a commitment I need to make."

"I understand."

"When do you go back to school?"

"Sunday morning." Stephen looked at his watch. "Morty, I have to go. I want to spend some time with my mother before my father gets home from work."

"It was great seeing you. Will you be home for Passover?"

"Not sure. We don't do anything for it anyway."

Morty averted his gaze from Stephen, not wanting him to feel he was being judgmental.

"You know how he is," Stephen said.

"Yes, mine is pretty much the same. At least he's agreed to let me make a *Seder* this year." Morty hesitated for a moment. "You should come. Bring your mother."

Stephen chuckled. "Perhaps. I'm not sure she would defy my father that way."

"It's odd the way they act, considering how they survived. You would think it would be important to them, all of them."

"Or perhaps not, for exactly that reason." Stephen rose from the table. "But it's important to you, so…you're doing something about it."

Stephen walked home alone along Bennett Avenue at a rapid pace, faster than he would normally have. He needed this time alone with his mother. She had finally agreed to tell him the things his father would not, what their life had been in Europe before they fled, how they had come to Sosúa, and then here to the United States. He needed to know. His father wouldn't discuss it. "The past is dead. It shouldn't concern you," he would say, whenever Stephen asked.

As he neared 189th Street he saw the young woman from the cafeteria again, the Rabbi's daughter. One of the children was on the sidewalk and crying. She was crouched over him, the folds of her dark green skirt surrounding her like a flowing robe. Her delicate hand caressed the child's cheek, comforting him. His pant leg was torn, and there was blood on the boy's knee and the sidewalk.

Stephen crossed the street, his heart racing a bit. He was shy around girls to begin with. He didn't have his father's ability to flirt and charm, an attribute that he often found embarrassing when his father, and his European friends, became too flirtatious with other women in front of their wives.

"Do you need some help?" Stephen asked, the words nearly catching in his throat.

Rachel looked up at him. She blushed slightly. He looked into her eyes. They were the color of a stormy sky on a wintry day. Her skin was a pale pink, her face framed by her rich, dark hair. The collar of her sweater, which matched the color of her eyes, covered her neck entirely.

"Yes, perhaps," she said. "Thank you. I can't carry him." She sighed and shook her head. "He was running ahead and didn't listen when I told him to stop. He caught his shoe on the tree there." She pointed to the gnarled root pushing up between the sections of concrete sidewalk. Stephen glanced at the protruding root, and then at the heavy, old-fashioned, leather shoes the boy wore. Sneakers would have been much better for running around. The boy was lighter than Stephen expected. "Where are we going," he asked, straightening up, the boy in his arms.

Rachel pointed up Bennett Avenue. "To the *shul*, I mean synagogue."

Stephan smiled. "I know what that means."

Rachel blushed again. "You're Jewish?"

"Yes."

Stephen followed Rachel, carrying the boy up Bennett Avenue to the corner of West 186th Street. "Wait here, please," she said. She ran into the synagogue and came back with another man who took the boy from Stephen.

"Go with Shmuely," Rachel said to the other children. When they were inside, she turned to Stephen. "Thank you. I'm sorry, I didn't ask your name."

"Stephen, Stephen Redmond," he said and extended his hand to her. She slipped her hand into the pocket of her skirt.

"I apologize. I suppose I should know that."

Rachel smiled. "That's okay. Why would you?"

Stephan hesitated a moment. "I saw you at the 'Y' today. I wanted to meet you."

"I guess that was *HaShem's* plan."

Stephen wasn't sure exactly what that meant. "I live right there." He pointed to 105 Bennett. "I hope we meet again some time."

Rachel averted her eyes, but Stephen noticed the corner of her mouth curled up into a smile.

Chapter 8
Washington Heights, NYC
4 August 2008
4:30 p.m.

Tolya and Pete stood in front of Erno's apartment at 790 Ft. Washington Avenue. "*Momento,*" came a woman's voice from inside. A moment later, Anisa opened the door. Her hands in rubber gloves, she held a bottle of glass cleaner and a rag in her left hand. "Detective, is señor Enrique expecting you?"

"No." Tolya smiled his most boyish, endearing grin. "Anisa, this is my partner, Pedro Gonzalvez."

"*Encantado,*" Pete said.

Anisa looked Pete up and down. She frowned. "Come in, please. And wipe your feet. Señor Enrique, you have visitors," she called out. "You know the way," she said, disappearing into the small corridor that led to the kitchen.

Tolya led Pete down the long hallway toward the living room. He stopped about three quarters of the way and pointed to a framed photo on the wall. Pete looked at it hard then nodded. "Yeah, that's them." He chuckled. "That's some memory you got, Tol."

Erno was seated in his wheelchair next to the ornate, brocade couch. The hem of the lace curtains that covered the window rested on the couch's back. Sunlight broke through the blinds in streaks. Though the room was warm, even with the air conditioner on, Erno wore a long-sleeve cardigan over his white shirt, which was buttoned to the top. His skin was nearly translucent, but he still retained a thick head of white hair. When he saw Tolya he smiled, bringing his whole being back to life. "Detective, how good to see you."

"Thank you, *señor*. Do you remember my partner?"

"Yes, of course, from your son's *bris*."

Pete shook Erno's hand. It was warm despite his age. "Nice to see you again, *señor*."

"What an unexpected pleasure. I'm afraid I don't have much to offer you, though. I don't get out much." A smile crept up Erno's lips, his self-deprecation endearing. "Would you like a cold drink?"

"Just water," Tolya said.

Erno's gaze shifted to Pete.

"Me too, thanks."

"*Anisa, dos vasos de agua, por favor*," Erno said, his voice strong, despite his obvious frailness.

"May we sit down?" Tolya asked.

"Of course."

They maneuvered around the heavy wood coffee table to the couch. It would have been a tight fit for either of them alone. For both, it was nearly impossible.

Erno smiled. "Detectives, you're smart boys, why not push the coffee table forward. Get comfortable."

Tolya found himself as charmed as always by the old man's accent, impossible to place, but pleasant to listen to. "We don't want to mess up your living room."

Anisa returned with their waters. She put the small tray on which they sat on the credenza near the hallway, scowling, she pulled the heavy coffee table forward away from the couch with little effort then placed a glass in front of each one of them. "I put some ice," she said, turning and leaving as abruptly as she had entered, clearly irritated by their unexpected intrusion into her daily routines.

"Very capable woman," Pete said, sipping his water.

"Quite," replied Erno, his expression filled with comical mischief. "Before you tell me why you're here Tolya, tell me about your beautiful wife, and little Max," his eyes widening, clearly happy to have company.

"They're both fine. He's growing fast." Tolya took out his phone and showed Erno a photo. "Karin is pregnant again."

Erno smiled broadly, showing his still-white teeth. "That's wonderful. When is the baby due?"

"The end of September."

"Is it a boy or a girl?"

"Another boy."

"Perhaps I will be at the *bris*."

"I hope so," replied Tolya.

Erno looked off into the shadows in the hallway, drifting off for a moment, somewhere far away. He mumbled something inaudibly, then looked back to Tolya. "Now, tell me what I can do for you."

Tolya looked over at Pete and hesitated. He was more uncomfortable than he'd imagined he would be. "*Señor*, we find ourselves in a really odd position."

Erno smiled. "Detective, what are you talking about? I'm a very old man. You'd best get to the point while I'm still alive."

Pete laughed. "My grandmother used to say something very similar."

"We found a body in a very peculiar place," Tolya said.

"And that's what you came to tell me? I'm honored. You didn't need that excuse to come for a visit."

Tolya accepted Erno's banter as just that, the delight of a solitary old man at having someone to banter with. "This body was buried in a wall on the third floor of an old wood frame house at 669 West 187th Street."

Erno fell silent. Pete pulled a copy of the title history from his pocket. "Are you Ernest Eisen?"

"I was," Erno said.

"You owned that house with Max Rothman?" Tolya asked.

"I did."

"Do you know anything about that body?" Pete asked.

"I do."

"What specifically," Pete said, leaning forward from the couch.

"I put it there," Erno said, the same broad, welcoming smile on his face as when they walked into the room.

The Captain nodded his head, his lips pursed, as Tolya told him about their interview with Erno. "We will have to bring him in for an interrogation and a statement."

"Cap, we really gonna arrest a ninety-nine-year-old man for a murder that happened like about forty years ago?" Pete protested.

"I don't see that we have any choice. He confessed to a murder."

Tolya glanced over at Pete. Yes, Erno had confessed, but there had to be some other way. Dragging the old man into the precinct was overkill. "Captain, perhaps we don't have to bring him in," he said. "It's not like he's a flight risk. How would you feel about us doing an interview in his apartment? We can have someone from the D.A.'s office present, a stenographer if you really think it's necessary. According to his caregiver, he hasn't left the apartment in nearly a year."

The Captain considered what Tolya said. "The two of you thought this all out before you came in to see me, didn't you?"

"Yep," Pete replied, nodding. "We also considered not telling you at all." ·

The Captain laughed. "Smartass," he replied, then hesitated for a moment. "Okay. Here's what I want you to do. I agree, this could turn into a circus real fast. Bringing him here could create other problems. Forget the D.A for now. Go take his statement and then we will see where we go with this. I'm not sure there's much point anyway. He's likely to die long before he ends up on trial."

Tolya turned on the video camera and spoke slowly. "This is the interview of Henrique Hierron, also known as

Ernest Eisen, in connection with the death and disappearance of Fernando Vargas in July of nineteen-sixty-six. Mr. Hierron has confessed to concealing the body of Mr. Vargas in the wall of the back bedroom on the third floor of the house located at 669 West 187th Street." Tolya placed the microphone on the small table next to Erno's chair then sat down next to Pete on the couch. Erno was perched in his wheelchair, wearing the same white shirt as earlier, but now with a knitted wool blanket covering him up to his chest in place of the green cardigan. He hair was slightly a mess as well. Anisa had woken him from his nap when they arrived.

"Please state your name for the record?" Tolya said into the microphone, then moved it closer to Erno. He checked the recording volume to make sure it was at its highest level.

"Henrique Hierron," Erno replied. He coughed slightly, clearing his throat.

"Have you ever been known by any other name?"

"Yes, several."

"Was one of them Ernest Eisen?" Pete asked.

"Yes."

"Let the record show that the name on the transfer of the deed for the property located at 669 West 187th Street contains that same name, Ernest Eisen," Pete said.

"Did you once own the property located at 669 West 187th Street, County of New York, State of New York?" Tolya asked.

"Yes."

"Who was your partner in the ownership of that property?"

"Max Rothman,"

"Was he known by any other names?"

"Yes, Max Redmond and Máximo Rothman."

"When did you buy the property with Mr. Rothman?"

Erno thought for a moment. "It was in nineteen-fifty-five. I was still living in Sosúa, in the Dominican Republic. Max had the opportunity to buy the property. He wrote to me and asked me to come here and go into business with him. He wanted to open a rooming house. That was his business many years before, in Europe, before the war."

"Was that your business too?" Pete asked.

"No," Erno said with a chuckle. "Not at all. Before the war I was mostly a bon-vivant living in Budapest, the only son of a wealthy doctor. My parents died young and I inherited a lot of money. I spent most of it on booze, and women, and gambling." Erno smiled, remembering. His eyes lit up, then clouded over again, just as suddenly, the happy memory metamorphosing into another, terrifying instead. "I used what money I had left to escape with my wife from Europe. I was a very wealthy communist and the fascists were after me. Eventually, we landed in Santo Domingo, which is where I met Max, in Sosúa, a refugee settlement near Puerto Plata. My wife and I weren't cut out for a life of farming, though. When Max offered to bring us to the United States we jumped at the prospect."

"What year did you come?"

"Nineteen-fifty-five."

Pete checked the deed. The transfer date to Max Rothman and Ernest Eisen was November 3, 1955. He looked at the sales price of the building, $25,000. There was no recorded mortgage. The purchase was for all cash. "If you don't mind me asking," Pete said, "where did two poor guys like you get that kind of money. That was a lot of cash back then?"

Erno's translucent skin somehow took on a gray tone. His face became angry. "Reparations. The Germans were forced to pay us our blood money."

Tolya glanced at Pete, delaying the questioning for a moment, giving Erno a chance to steady himself. He hadn't meant to drag Erno back to those times but realized now that it was inevitable.

"How did you come to meet Fernando Vargas?" Tolya asked, trying to move the time frame and subject matter of the interrogation forward.

"We met him in a Latin night club."

Pete smiled at the thought of Erno and Max out for a night of dancing and drinking. His smile caught Erno's eye. Erno smiled back at him, the change in the focus of his personal history moving back to happier memories again, from pre-war Europe and its Nazis to a Caribbean nightclub in the 60's in New York City, cleared the terror those earlier years still generated. "That amuses you, Detective?" Erno asked.

"Well, I know how much Dominicans love a good nightclub. I guess even back then. And you both lived in Santo Domingo for a long time."

"Yes," Erno chuckled, remembering again, these memories charmed and charming, not chilling and haunting like those that had grabbed him moments earlier. "We both developed a taste for Latin…um…music down there." He winked at Pete. "Especially Max. He loved anything Dominican. The food, the music…you know. We would go to dance every now and then after we came here. Just to remember."

"With your wives?" Pete asked.

"Sometimes." Erno winked again. "Not always."

Pete exchanged a knowing glance with Erno.

"Okay," said Tolya. "That's enough with the homeboy stuff. Let's get back to this."

"Of course, Detective," said Erno, turning back to Tolya. The memories of those times with Max had sparked some feeling of life in him. They seemed to impart an energy that changed him, picked him up. "What would you like to know?"

"How did Vargas come to live at the rooming house?"

"As I said, we met him at Las Palmas, that was the name of the club. It was originally a Cuban club, but by nineteen-sixty-five there were a good number of Dominicans living in the neighborhood. Mostly political refugees from Trujillo and then alternatively from the Bosch government. The club owners knew that, so they would have a merengue night once a week, usually Friday and everyone would go. We were at the bar one night and Vargas was standing next to us. We began talking with him. He said he needed a room. We had one. It was less money than the room he had downtown, so he moved in."

Tolya didn't glance over to Pete. He didn't want Erno to suspect they had any other version of events. He made a mental note of the differences in Erno's version of the story from Miriam Rivera's. He and Pete would discuss that later. "You were friends, then?"

"At the beginning, yes."

"What happened afterward?" Pete asked.

Erno hesitated. "He didn't pay his rent on time."

Tolya leaned back against the couch, flabbergasted. "That's it? He ended up dead inside the wall because he didn't pay his rent on time?"

"No," Erno said. "He ended up dead in a wall because he pulled a gun on us."

"When did that happen?"

"July fourth, nineteen-sixty-six, late in the evening." Erno's eyes assumed that far-away look again, remembering. His face became sad. "Max had come to get me and help me close-up for the night. We were going to meet our wives at a party and to see some fireworks in Fort Tryon Park. Vargas came in and went up to his room. At that time, he owed us two weeks' rent. We heard a racket coming from his room, so we went upstairs. He was packing his things, throwing everything into his two suitcases. He said he was leaving. He was going with his girlfriend to Miami. We asked him for the rent money he owed us. He pulled a gun from his pants, from his waist in the back."

Tolya glanced at Pete, raising one eyebrow. "And then what happened?"

"He said he wasn't going to pay us anything. He said he'd shoot both of us and disappear before the police found our bodies. He pointed the gun at Max's chest." Erno moved his shoulders slightly forward. "I lunged at him and grabbed the gun. I couldn't let him hurt Max. Max was like my brother. He brought me to America. He had a child. If anyone was to die, it would have to be me."

"And this was in Vargas' room?" Tolya said.

"Yes."

"Which room was his room?" Pete asked.

"On the third floor in the back."

"Did the gun go off?"

"Not then, no. As I told you, I lunged for the gun and grabbed the nozzle. I was bigger than Vargas, stronger. I turned the pistol to his gut and then the gun went off. I forced his finger down on the trigger. It tore a hole in his stomach."

"No one heard anything?" Tolya asked.

"Amazingly, no. The neighborhood kids were lighting fireworks in the streets at that time and the gun shot blended in. It was the Fourth of July, after all. Independence Day."

"Did he die right there?" Tolya asked.

"Pretty much. There was blood everywhere. We didn't know what to do with the body. Neither of us had any experience with a thing like this."

"Why did you put him in the wall?" Pete asked.

Erno thought for a moment. "Honestly detectives, I don't really remember. It all happened very fast. We needed to make the body disappear."

"Why didn't you go to the police?"

Erno laughed. "Two immigrants Jews with the dead body of a Dominican in a pool of blood? Would you?" With that Erno began to cough, ending the interview.

Neither Tolya nor Pete said anything until they were on the street. At the curb in front of the building Tolya said, "He's lying."

"Absolutely," said Pete. "Question is, why would he lie now?"

"He's covering for someone."

"But who? It's been over 40 years?" Pete waited a moment for Tolya's response. He got none. "Do you really want to pursue this, Tol?"

Tolya shook his head. "Yeah, I think so."

"To what purpose?" Pete asked. He would humor Tolya if solving this case was that important to him.

"I need to know. We need to know. It doesn't matter who the victim was, or how old Erno is. A crime was committed, a murder was committed. It's our job to find out why."

"Okay then, what do you propose we do?"

Tolya thought for a moment. "What did we do with all those diaries when we solved the Redmond murder?"

"I think I sent all that down to be filed as part of the evidence. Yeah, I'm sure I did as I think about it. The son didn't want any of it."

"Let's get those diaries."

Chapter 9
Washington Heights, NYC
5 August 2008
9:30 a.m.

Shalom read the essay in front of him for the third time. He was very impressed with this student. At only 12 years of age, not yet a Bar-Mitzvah, the boy had a clear understanding of the conflicting concepts of God's will vs. individual decisions taken clearly in contradiction to God's laws. It was the single issue that had made Shalom *Baal t'shuva*. It had haunted him for ten years before he finally came to some peace with it, and himself. That peace, the result of many conversations with the man who would become his father-in-law, led him back to the Judaism his father had abandoned.

Shalom still struggled to understand his father's rejection of, and animosity toward, Judaism. He also knew how much it had hurt his mother. She had tried, despite his father's determination to spare Shalom from the disappointment of faith, to instill in him some sense of pride and whatever knowledge she could give him without his father knowing. She was thankful to *HaShem* when Shalom returned to the faith, despite Max's anger with him.

Shalom got up from his desk and went to the mahogany credenza that sat against the wall on the left side of the room. He opened the middle drawer and removed an old three-ring binder. On the cover of the blue binder was a sticker marked in both English and Yiddish: Essays on Free Choice. Underneath was the name of the author, Abraham Schoenweiss. Shalom sat down at his desk and opened it. The essay he sought was near the end. It was written in Yiddish. An English translation was immediately behind it. Shalom would make a copy of both for his young student with a special note. In the meantime, he began to read it again to understand the deep significance it had held for Rabbi Schoenweiss, its author.

Washington Heights, NYC
July 1975

Helen pushed the knot of the tie up gently around Stephen's shirt collar. She straightened the collar, put her hands on Stephen's cheeks, and kissed him softly on the forehead.

"There, how handsome you look."

Stephen stared at himself in the mirror. People, usually his parents' friends or the relatives, told him how handsome he was. He couldn't see it and didn't believe it. While he had his father's fair coloring and chestnut hair, blue eyes, and high cheekbones, he knew he lacked his charm and confidence. While Max was the center of the room at any gathering, easy and relaxed with both men and women, Stephen was shy and reserved, more like his mother. The man he stared at in the mirror was ordinary. He hadn't crossed continents or oceans, nor had he subdued a jungle.

"Remember," his mother said, "be yourself."

"I don't know their customs."

"They're not that complicated." She took his hand. "Just follow what they do. If you're unsure, ask. They will accept you for you."

Stephen smiled. "Thank you, mother."

"There's nothing to thank me for."

Stephen hesitated. "Where's dad?"

Helen took a breath. "He's in the living room. He woke from his nap while you were dressing. Don't worry, I've spoken to him. He won't say anything more."

"I still don't understand. Why does he hate them so?"

Helen sighed. "I've told you. Too much happened. Too many things all at once. He asked God for help once and God didn't help him. I've never understood if he resents God for that or just doesn't believe God exists. He feels they're all hypocrites, these people, particularly those that didn't experience what we lived through."

"If he would just talk about it. Talk to me about it. I want to understand."

"It's too painful to him."

Shalom felt a pang of pain shoot through him. His father wasn't the only one who was damaged by his history. It had affected Stephen deeply as well. His parents' trauma permeated his mind every day. He looked at the clock on the night table beside his bed. "I'd best go."

"Yes, I remember how they like to start *Shabbos* early," said Helen. "My father was like that."

Stephen took a step toward the door. He tried to imagine the man in the photograph who was his mother's father moving about, talking, making *Shabbos*. He wanted to ask her about him. What was he like? Was he, Stephen, anything like him? But he didn't. He'd asked before, too many times. His mother could talk about the events of her life, their escape, their life in Sosúa, but she could never talk about her parents, or her brothers and sisters. That left a huge hole in Stephen's understanding of the world. If she tried to talk about them the conversation would inevitably turn to tears, and the tears to weeping, then the weeping to a panic attack, all within moments. "You never miss it, mama?" was all he could muster.

"There are times when I do. But for me it's the past. I made a choice. I chose your father. And from that choice I have you." She put her hands on his cheeks again and pushed herself up on her toes to kiss him gently. "It's a small sacrifice when I think of it that way."

Stephen didn't really understand the conflation of her marriage and his birth with the abandonment of her family traditions, but he left it alone. He touched his mother's hand, a touch so light she barely felt it, then walked down the hall to the front door. As he passed the living room, his father, seated in his big club chair, was smoking one of his cigarillos. Stephen stopped for a moment. "Have a good evening, papa."

His father looked at him. He avoided Stephen's eyes. "You too," he said, then picked up the newspaper and hid behind it.

Rachel's father made a blessing over the wine. He chanted in a pleasant, sincere voice. Stephen had no idea what the words of the prayer meant, but he felt something akin to joy as the Rabbi finished, everyone at the table responded Amen and took a sip of their wine.

"Thank you for joining us," the Rabbi said as they sat down.

"Thank you for inviting me," Stephen replied. He glanced at Rachel sitting opposite him. She lowered her eyes. A pale, pink blush rose into her cheeks. "Excuse me," she said. "I'm going to help mother in the kitchen."

Stephen was alone with the Rabbi. He felt a knot form in his throat. He had no idea what to talk to this man about. His beard and clothing were so different than the casual dress and carefully barbered appearance of his father and his father's friends, that Stephen felt like he had been transported to a different country in an earlier time. His eyes took in the room, thick with breakfronts constructed of dark wood and filled with china and silver pieces and bookcases packed with volume upon volume of books, all the titles printed in the Hebrew alphabet. He searched for something to say.

"My daughter tells me you live across the street from our *shul*," said the Rabbi, breaking the uncomfortable silence.

"Yes," Stephen said, clasping his hands on the edge of the table in front of him. He noticed a slight accent to the Rabbi's speech.

"Have you lived there long?"

"All my life."

The Rabbi hesitated for a moment. "Does your family belong to a *shul*? The Jewish Center on Fort Washington Avenue?"

Stephen swallowed hard. "No, Rabbi. I'm afraid they don't. We don't. They, well mostly my father, doesn't believe in anything."

"But you are Jewish?"

"Yes."

"They were born here. In this country?"

"Stephen shook his head. "No."

"May I ask where?"

"They're Hungarian. The towns where they lived are in Czechoslovakia now."

The Rabbi tore off a small piece from the *challah* he had blessed earlier and bit into it. He closed his eyes for a moment before continuing his questioning. "Did they go to the camps?"

"No," replied Stephen. "They escaped to the Dominican Republic. Their families died in the camps, though."

The Rabbi nodded. "I see. We escaped before the war too. Nearly the whole community. We came from Germany. I was an infant when we came here."

"The soup is ready," said Rachel, entering the dining room carrying a large tureen. She placed it in the center of the table and uncovered it. The warm, rich fragrance of chicken broth filled the room. Matzah balls floated on top, garnished with chopped, fresh dill. "May I serve you, papa?"

The Rabbi smiled and handed his plate to Rachel. "Thank you."

Rachel ladled two matzah balls and some of the clear, golden broth into the flower-patterned, gold-rimmed china bowl. She placed it back to the Rabbi's waiting hands. "May I serve you?" she asked Stephen.

He looked at Rachel's serene face. She was the most beautiful girl he had ever seen. "Please," he replied, handing her his bowl.

"One or two?" she asked.

He looked at her, his lack of understanding clear.

"Matzah balls," Rachel added, giggling self-consciously.

Stephen felt his cheeks redden. He smiled. How foolish he was. "Two, please."

Rachel carefully ladled the soup and matzah balls into Stephen's bowl. "Thank you," he said, taking it.

"Good appetite," the Rabbi said, slicing into one of his matzah balls with his soup spoon. "Perfect. Light and fluffy, as always."

The rest of the meal was as delicious as the matzah balls—roasted chicken, egg barley with mushrooms, green beans with carrots. It was also pleasant and engaging. Rabbi Schoenweiss spoke about the community and his dedication to it. Their history went back nearly 1,000 years. They weren't going to allow anyone or anything, not even the Nazis, to destroy their past or their future. They were thriving right here on Bennett Avenue. For the first time in his life Stephen encountered refugee Jews who had had a different experience than his parents and their friends. These Jews remained Jews. They mourned those they had lost, but at the same time kept their special relationship with God.

Stephen's father and many of his friends had rejected God and Judaism out of anger. They might claim it was out of disappointment, or as a result of being rudely awakened to the truth, but it was clear now to Stephen, their rejection was born of rage. They had a right to be angry, this he didn't deny, but one could be angry and also forgive, even one's self.

"May I ask you something quite personal?" Rabbi Schoenweiss said after his wife and daughter had left the room to attend to dessert.

"If it's about me and your daughter..."

"No, it's not,' the Rabbi replied. "Not directly, anyway."

Stephen felt a nervous twitch in his stomach. "Of course," he said, despite his unease with the question.

"Do you believe that *HaShem* controls everything or does he give man the option to make choices, whether those choices be right or wrong?"

Stephen chose his words carefully. His mother had warned him, the Rabbi might want to engage in a philosophical discussion after the meal. It was common practice among the orthodox. Her father, and her brothers, and grandfathers, often did. He didn't want to insult Rachel's father. "I really can't say," he replied. "I am embarrassed to tell you I've never studied Jewish thought. I've never studied Jewish anything. I have no idea what Jewish teaching says about that. Why do you ask?"

Rabbi Schoenweiss smiled. "I will answer your question in a moment. First, another question. Would you like to study?"

"Yes," Stephen answered. He was surprised by how quickly the word popped out of his mouth.

The Rabbi smiled. "I ask because I believe we have both. *HaShem* commands us to do certain *mitzvot*. We can choose to do them or not to. We can choose not even to believe in *HaShem*. We have that will. But I also believe *HaShem* puts us on the right path if he believes we have a pure heart."

"And if we don't?"

"He may let us follow the path of evil. Nothing good will ever come of it and we will know his displeasure. Judaism is about what we do, not what we feel."

Chapter 10
Washington Heights, NYC
5 August 2008
5:30 p.m.

Pete dropped the evidence box on the desk. "Don't you think it's a little strange that the son didn't want any of these, back?"

"Who knows," Tolya replied. "Sometimes people just want to forget, or not be reminded. And besides, storage space is at a premium in New York apartments."

They both laughed, but then Pete became deadly serious. "You'd think a man would keep something his father had written. I wish I had something, anything, from my father."

Tolya frowned. "Maybe you're right. I didn't keep a thing either though, now I'm sorry. But, lucky for us," he said pointing to the box. "I think we split these up by language, Spanish for you, English for me."

Tolya took the thin, leather-bound volumes out of the box one by one checking each for their language and date. There were twelve notebooks dated from 1950 to 1966. He removed the ones they had read during the Máximo Rothman murder investigation. Of those remaining, three were in Spanish and eight in English. One was in another language altogether. Tolya studied it. "Looks like Hungarian again, there were a couple others like that last time."

"And who are we going to get to translate that?" Pete said. "Last time Erno did it. He's already confessed. We can't have him reviewing the evidence."

"True. In the meantime, take these three and take two of the English volumes as well. Have a fun night!"

ↄ◌ↄ

Pete settled into the club chair in his living room and turned on the lamp. It was 11:30. Glynnis and all the kids were in bed, asleep. He skimmed through the five notebooks and found the one with the earliest date, March 1950. The Spanish was nearly perfect and sprinkled with purely Dominican expressions. He was impressed with Max Rothman. Max had literally become Dominican, not a small task in Pete's estimation. Dominican-ness was something one was born to. Max's transformation was clear in both his choice of language and his thoughts. Pete began reading, speaking the words almost inaudibly to himself.

"As I look out at the sea, I am packing our kitchen. The sadness is more than I can bear. I can't leave this place, but I can't stay either. It's too much of me: my life, those I love, and have loved, remain here. Merengue is playing on the radio. The rhythm matches the gentle waves as I watch them caress the shore from our window."

Pete took a deep breath. He felt himself choke up a little. Only a Dominicano puro could feel this way, understand this emotion. Pete missed home every day, no matter how long he was in New York. He looked down at the page and began again, slowly deciphering the elegant, European script.

"I would stay, but the pressure on us is overwhelming. Guilt more than I can bear. My brother has begged me. He is alone, I'm all he has left. Helen's nephew berates her. His parents are dead, his brother and sisters gone as well. He has no one else. Neither do we. They are all gone, to the last, up in smoke.

She wants to go. I want to stay. But on the other hand, my life here haunts me as well. Anabela is never far from my thoughts, nor José. They walk with me every day. If I leave here, I fear their spirits will abandon me to remain here in this place, forever. But if Helen and I are to have a life, to begin a life together again, we must leave. This place is at once a magnet to my heart, but, too full of ghosts, haunting my every step. Sadly, when I arrive in New York, these ghosts that I love and hold near to me every day will be replaced by other ghosts, ghosts I can't yet face."

Pete put the thin notebook down in his lap for a moment. He looked at the time, midnight. He felt as if Max words were his words. They spoke to the loss he felt when he left Santo Domingo. No one leaves there easily.

March 7, 1950
Sosúa, Dominican Republic

I walked slowly on the narrow path through the forest that led to the tiny village where I had lived with José, his family, and Anabela. I hadn't been there for some time, the memories were too vivid and too painful even now, so many years later. Nevertheless, I had to say a proper and private goodbye. As I neared the village the scent of roasting meat met my senses, as always. I half expected José to be standing near the fire, shirtless, the way he was all those years ago, nearly ten years now, when I first started coming here. I hesitated a moment, my eyes tearing and my throat choking from my memories. Those six months living here were the best of my life. If I had only listened to José we all might still be here, together.

I spotted José's house across the small clearing at the center of the hamlet. Josécito stood on the porch repairing something. He didn't see me. He had grown to a man in the years since José's death and looked exactly like him, of medium height with a powerful build and dark, even skin. He shaved his head, as José had.

Josécito turned. He stretched his arms above his head and scanned the view but still didn't see me coming. When he did, he smiled and waved, his smile José's. I picked up my pace and closed the distance between us quickly as Josécito walked the two steps down from the porch. I grabbed him and pulled him to me, embracing him for a long moment. "*Como tú 'ta?*" I asked. I realized how much I would miss the sound of Spanish.

"*Bien tío, y tú?*"

"I am well,"

"Why haven't we seen you? We miss you," Josécito said. "Why don't you come more often? Your room is waiting for you."

I couldn't tell him the truth quite yet. I would never sleep in that room again. "You know it's very difficult for me to get away now, because of the business," I lied. I had opened a small guest house near the beach, but it was rarely full and usually nearly empty. A woman appeared at the door of the wood house. "*Tío*," she said smiling as she walked down the two steps to greet me.

We embraced. "*Que bella eres*," I said. At 21, Camilia was more beautiful than ever. She reminded me of Anabela. She had the same color, coffee with cream, and the same eyes. Deep, dark, and seductive.

"*Gracias*," Camilia said. "You look well yourself. Come in, I will make you something to drink. Do you still like *guanabo*?"

"One does not stop liking *guanabo*," I replied. "Can we take it out here on the porch?"

"Of course," she said, disappearing into the house.

I preferred to stay outside. The ghosts were less visible. I sat down on the same bench where I used to sit with José to talk about everything and anything. I owed him so much. I wouldn't have survived those first few years without him.

Josécito sat down beside me. "How is *tía* Helen?" he asked.

"She's well. She's in charge of the guests today."

"Does she like it, having the guest house?"

"Well enough," I lied again. She hated the work. When we had a small hotel in Slovakia, before the war, she was managing the servants, not changing the linen.

"I have something to tell you *tío*."

"What's that *mijo*?"

"I have met a girl."

I smiled. Though he was barely eighteen, Josécito would soon marry and have his own family. The local people didn't wait for a future they would never have or conceive of. Their lives were dictated by the seasons and by the rhythms of life. A young man needed a young woman and they needed a family of their own. "Is she from this village?"

Josécito shook his head. "No, from the next." He pointed in the direction of Puerto Plata. Small encampments like this were strung out every mile or so till you reached the outskirts of the city.

"Is she beautiful?" I asked.

"Yes, very," Josécito said, staring off into the distance. Even with his dark skin one could see the blush rise in his cheeks.

I drew Josécito to me. "I am happy for you, *mijo*. I hope you find the same happiness that your parents had. What's her name?"

"Beatrix. I want you to meet her."

I knew that would never happen, but I smiled and said, "and I would like to know her, and someday your children."

"*Tío*," Camilia said. She handed a cup filled with light green juice to me.

"*Gracias*," I said, then took a sip. "*Rico*, exactly like your mother used to give me." I looked toward the fenced-in area about fifty meters to the left of the house.

"Would you like to visit them?" Camilia asked.

"Yes," I said. We walked hand in hand, Camilia, Josécito and me, to the tiny cemetery. Josécito opened the wrought iron gate. There was a new grave to the right, adorned only with a cross and a garland of flowers.

"Elizabeta died a couple weeks back," Camilia said. "She was nearly 100."

"I'll go to see her family before I leave," I said. "You should have contacted me."

Neither replied. We continued to the back of the little cemetery. In the corner, unlike on the other graves, was a small headstone engraved with two names and one fateful date. Underneath the date it said, 'In Life and In Love, Here and for Eternity."

I knelt at the gravesite and placed a pebble on the headstone, as was my custom. "Old friend," I said in a low voice. I felt my voice cracking and the tears well up in my eyes. "I have come to tell you something. I have come to say goodbye to you both."

Josécito and Camilia looked at me. "What are you saying, *tío*?"

I stood and took their hands in mine. "We are going to New York."

Josécito dropped my hand. "Why, *tío*?"

"I don't want to, but Helen was never happy here. You know we have no one."

"You have us," Camilia said, taking a small step back. I saw the tears in her eyes.

"I have you. Yes. But Helen has no one. Her nephew is there. He and my brother convinced her, and I owe her that much. I can't let her go alone."

Josécito and Camilia put their arms around me. "I understand," Camilia said. "When are you leaving?"

"Tomorrow. Give me a few moments alone with your parents, please."

I watched as Camilia and Josécito walked back to the house slowly, then knelt before the grave. I began to weep. "José, I am so sorry for what I did to you, for bringing this upon you. I could never have asked for a better friend. You were more than that, you were truly my brother. I should have listened to you. We should have fled. I will carry this guilt with me forever. Please forgive me. Please, forgive Máximo Rothman."

I took the small wooden box from my pocket that I had crafted myself in the carpentry shop in the settlement and scooped up some earth from the grave and placed it inside. I smiled. José would be so proud of me. I had learned to do everything a man needed to do to be independent: carpentry, farming, even to repair machinery. The clumsy immigrant from Europe had disappeared long ago, and with him the desire for the kind of life I was headed to. But what choice did I have now? I slid the box into my pocket and dried my eyes with the backs of my hands. I stood and walked to the house without looking back.

Josécito sat on the bench in that same spot that José loved so many years ago. I sat down beside him. "*Mijo*, I will miss you. I want to share something with you that your father told me a long time ago. He would tell you this if he were here."

Josécito looked into my eyes and smiled. "I miss him, them, every day, still."

"As do I." I put my hands on the boy's shoulders. He was sturdy like his father. "Treat Beatrix with love. That's all women really want, to feel loved. Be kind and appreciate everything she does for you every day, because she does it with love."

Josécito embraced me. He reached into his pocket and took out a photograph. "I want you to have this."

I looked at the black and white photo. It was taken on the beach in Sosúa on the day I told José I had made the decision to leave the settlement and move to the village to live with him and his family and Anabela. It was of Josécito with me, the ocean behind us. I was holding his hand. He was so little then. "I will keep this with me always," I said. "I will keep all of you in my heart, always."

The voyage by boat to New York took six days. It was the reverse of the voyage to Santo Domingo we had taken ten years earlier. In that grey month of December in 1940, the temperature had gotten gradually warmer as we moved southward. All we had was our heavy winter clothing. Now, as we sailed north, the temperatures dropped, and ironically, we, especially me, had nothing but tropical clothing. I had shed my *Mittleuropan* attire along with my *Mittleuropan* life. I wanted to fit in with the Dominicans themselves, not just for comfort. Embarrassingly, the only warm suit I had kept had not pants but nickers, which is what I now found myself dressed in.

We were processed quickly enough at Ellis Island. Unlike the last time, they welcomed us warmly. The weather was cold and the wind strong. I felt myself shiver for the first time after ten years in the Tropics.

We collected our bags from the pier, took the ferry over to Manhattan and found assistance from someone who spoke German to find a cab. I checked my jacket pocket again for the American money my brother had sent. It was there, as was the photo of Josécito with me on the beach in Sosúa.

"Pennsylvania Station," I said in heavily accented English, reading phonetically from the piece of paper Jack sent me some weeks ago with instructions."

"Okay," the driver said and headed into traffic.

I marveled at the buildings. Even Budapest paled in comparison to this great city. And the number of people on the street astounded me. Helen took my hand as I read the remaining instructions, which were in Hungarian. I was rusty with the language of my birth. But what else would Jack have written in? He didn't speak Spanish, and I didn't speak English. Hungarian was our mother tongue, our *lingua franca*. Yet, the words looked strange to me after so many years away from them.

"I'm so excited for our new life," Helen said. She leaned toward me and kissed me quickly and gently on the cheek. "But I'm a little apprehensive to see my nephew."

"I understand," I said. I smiled and kissed her back. "So am I. Too much has transpired. I don't want to talk to them about what happened."

In truth, I felt reticent at best. I barely remembered Jack. We had not seen each other in the ten years since we had stopped at Ellis Island on our way to Santo Domingo, and then it was only for a few minutes. I hadn't seen him for fifteen years before that, after he emigrated to the United States. I was doubly uncomfortable about accepting Jack's invitation to live with him and his family until we could establish ourselves. I had no idea what to expect, and that made me nervous.

The cab slowed and stopped in front of an imposing building. The taxi driver unloaded our bags. I looked at the meter and pulled some bills from my pocket and paid the driver. I read the note over again. Jack wrote to meet him under the stairs at the main ticketing area. His daughter Harriet would be with him. She was five years old the last time we saw her. Jack had sent pictures over the years. I knew she had red hair, like my sisters. Their memories flooded back at me; their ghosts already awakened. I took a deep breath. "Let's go," I said.

Helen was flustered trying to pick up one of the bags and keep hold of her handbag at the same time. "I'll take that, *drágám*," I said.

We walked into the station and down toward a large hall at the corridor's end, as per Jack's instructions and hand drawn map. There at the end of the corridor under a grand arch I saw a young woman with bright red hair. She had my sister Anna's face. For a moment, I felt my throat tighten. I had promised them I would bring them all to Santo Domingo, that I would save them. I had failed. Now they were gone, like so much smoke into the air, disappearing as it rose to the heavens. I walked up to the young woman, Helen a step or two behind. I wasn't sure what to feel. The young woman looked at me. She held a photo in her small, delicate hand. I noticed her staring at my knickers and felt embarrassed. The American men rushing by were dressed in modern, elegant suits with pants.

"Uncle Max?" the young woman said in Hungarian.

"*Egen*," I said. "*A jo napot*, Harriet," I replied, putting down the bags I held in each hand. Helen stood a half-step behind me. "It seems you have grown. Do you remember us?"

"Of course." She embraced me tightly. "We are so happy you have come. Both of you." She let go of me and embraced Helen.

"Where is your father?" I asked.

Harriet pointed across the room. A man with my face, but shorter than me, approached. "He wasn't sure what side of the station you would arrive on."

I smiled. "Just like Jack. He always has a plan."

❧❧❧

Pete put down the old diary and rubbed his eyes. He was moved both by Max's departure and arrival. It had dredged up his own memories. In the end, he knew that every immigrant experiences nearly the same thing, inconsolable loss, and at the same time, a chance to start again, to define your life for whatever you might want it to be.

Chapter 11
Washington Heights, NYC
5 August 2008
9:30 p.m.

Tolya pulled the six thin, dusty, leather-bound volumes from the plastic bag he had used to carry them from the station. He opened each looking for the date on the first page. They ranged from 1954 to 1966. "Do you think I should start with the oldest or the one closest to the murder date?" he asked Karin.

"I?" she said. "I think this is going to be we. I'm too invested in this story not to be involved in this." She reached across the coffee table and picked up one of the diaries, running her fingers gently across the top. The dust from the cover dirtied her fingertips.

Tolya smiled. He knew when not to challenge Karin. The diaries were evidence in a case, and technically she shouldn't be reading them. She was an ex-cop, and she knew that. He let it pass though, rather than fight with her, and reached for a tissue from the box on the end table. "Here," he said.

"Thanks," Karin kissed him lightly on his cheek. She cleaned the dirt off her fingers then dusted off the diaries.

"I think we should start with the oldest and work forward. We'll get a better feel for where his head was at."

Tolya sat back into the couch, spreading his legs. "And we're going to read this together?"

"Yes," Karin said, grinning broadly, her even, white, teeth filling her smile. "Out loud." She settled herself comfortably next to Tolya. "Would you like to read, or shall I?"

"You start," Tolya said. He wrapped his arm over her shoulder and pulled her closer.

Karin opened the first volume. It took her a moment to adjust to the flowing script.

"After five years here," she began, "I still find myself nostalgic for the climate in Santo Domingo. It's June, but I'm still wearing a sweater, especially at night. I laugh to myself, these people here, they're hot all the time. I never felt like that. I was born for the warmth.

I received a letter from Erno today. He's managing the dairy co-op now, but Sosúa has changed much. Many people have left. They've gone to Miami, a few to New York or New Jersey. The farms do well, and the co-op is profitable. Ava is well. She misses us. We miss them too. The truth is we've made a few friends here, but it's very hard, considering our experiences. These American Jews, they don't have any real understanding of what happened to us, only embarrassment concealed by pity. As to those who survived the camps, well, they are far worse off than we are. We can only imagine their nightmare. They live it all day, every day, awake or asleep.

Helen drags me to the synagogue up on Ft. Washington Avenue for social events. She wants me to go to prayer on

Shabbos. I smile and say no, inside I'm exploding. I don't understand how she can even think of that after everything that's happened. It wasn't bad enough that their so-called God took our families. He took our child as well. And what about the three pregnancies she lost since then, one there and two here. Thank God, she appears to be well enough with this one, but I don't want to ask for bad luck. We've had enough already. She's due in three weeks."

Karin put her hand on her stomach and stroked it, hoping the baby inside would feel her tender caress. She looked up into Tolya's face. "She's pregnant, again."

Washington Heights, NYC
July 1954

I walked slowly from the subway enjoying the evening's warmth. I was tired from the day's work. My job at the Hotel Paramount kept me inside for most of the day. The hotel had purchased one of these new air-cooling machines, an air conditioner I believe it's called, and by the time my shift was over I was nearly frozen. I walked the thirteen blocks to the subway station at Columbus Circle, rather than back the few blocks to 42nd Street, just to warm up a bit.

No matter, I had the several days off for Independence Day, and Helen is due the day after tomorrow, July 3rd. Just the mention of Independence Day brought back too many memories. Of course, it was a different Independence Day, February 27th, Dominican Independence Day, but nonetheless, it was Anabela who was in my mind. As I unlocked the front door to our apartment, I knew I had to stop thinking of her if Helen and I were ever to have a life. Helen was standing by the kitchen. She held a white towel in her hand. It was wet, a large, pinkish, stain discoloring part of it. Her expression betrayed her fear.

"My water broke," she said, her voice trembling.

My mind raced. The past rushed back at me. The disaster at our homestead. The miscarriage at the settlement. The two miscarriages here, particularly the one when Harriet was watching her after the doctor had sent her to bed in the seventh month. But this was different. Her due date was two days away. "Did you call the doctor?"

"Not yet. It just happened."

I ran down the hall to the small table near the entrance to the living room and grabbed the phone's handset. "I can't remember the number," I shouted.

"It's on the pad under the phone," Helen called back.

I grabbed the pad and dialed, the headset under my chin. My hand was shaking so badly I could barely see the number.

"Dr. Tamus' office," came the voice at the other end of the line.

"Uh, this is Max Redmond. My wife's water broke."

"That's good Mr. Redmond."

"But she's not due for another two days. The doctor said she would…"

"Not to worry, Mr. Redmond. The doctor will meet you at Bronx Lebanon Hospital in an hour."

"How will I get there?" I asked.

"Take a cab."

When Doctor Tamus handed me my son I was in a fog. I waited in the father's room with my brother and my sister-in-law for fourteen hours. The delivery was slow, the doctors had to be careful considering Helen's history. They wanted everything to turn out well. The nurse came and asked me to come into the delivery room. She wasn't smiling. I wasn't sure what was happening. I was terrified that something had gone wrong. I found Helen propped up on pillows, something wrapped in blankets in her arms.

Her face was covered with sweat. She smiled at me weakly. Her expression was one of exhaustion coupled with sheer joy. "Here is your son," she said.

I took the child tentatively in my arms.

"Support his head," the nurse said, her expression dour.

I looked down at his tiny face. At that moment I knew absolute, unconditional love. There was nothing that would ever be too much for me to do for this tiny being. He was from me and from Helen, he was us together. But he was more. He was all that we had lost, he was the resolution of our anger and disappointment. He was our future. "Welcome, *mijo*," I whispered in his tiny ear then kissed his cheek. I placed him gently and carefully back into Helen's arms. I kissed her tenderly, lingering for a moment on her lips. "Thank you," I said.

"There is nothing to thank me for," Helen replied. "I love you."

"What have you decided to name him?" Jack asked. We sat in the coffee shop on the first floor of the hospital. There wasn't much room in the maternity ward, and I needed a coffee.

"After Istvan, but in English. Stephen."

Jack nodded his head. I knew he wasn't happy about my choice. "I understand. And perhaps our father's name for his middle name?"

I hesitated for a moment. We had become close in the years since Helen and I arrived from Sosúa. Our lack of closeness before that was neither his fault nor mine. It was a matter of time and distance. He was much older than me to begin with, thirteen years. I held tender memories of him from my early childhood, then he went off to the war, and then to America. Still, there were things too private for discussions, my son's name among them. But he had found us Dr. Tamus, and without Tamus this never would have happened.

"I don't know Jack. I have to speak to Helen. She lost everyone too."

He smiled. "I understand, I was just asking. I'm sorry."

"No need to be."

He sipped at his coffee. He drank it black rather than use the milk in the hospital's restaurant without knowing for certain that it was kosher.

"Did you want to have the *bris* at our house? It's larger than your apartment and Charlotte could prepare the food."

I took a deep breath. I wasn't sure what to say to my brother, how to explain this to him. The subject was avoided too often. I accepted and respected his faith. He couldn't accept or respect my lack of it.

I intended to have Stephen circumcised. I wouldn't go that far, so as not to do it. Besides, Helen would insist upon it. But we could have it done in the hospital. It was a common enough practice these days, even among non-Jews. I didn't want to offer my son up to their god, not after what their god had taken from me. I no longer believed, I never would, and I wasn't a hypocrite.

"Let me ask Helen," I said again, avoiding the truth.

∽∾∽

"Max, please," said Helen. "I understand, I was there with you. He was my son as well. I lost my family too. But we are still Jews."

"Perhaps you feel that way," I replied.

Helen drew tiny Stephen closer to her. She stroked his forehead and then kissed it. "You can name him for your brother, that's fine. You can even give him your father's name as well, if that will bring you peace, or another of your brother's names, but I have to insist on this. My son will have a proper *bris*. He is a Jew, like me, and like it or not, like you."

I felt the anger run up into my chest, but I held myself back. I would never accept this evil god who punished for no reason. Or perhaps, as I realized that day, as the dawn broke over the tops of the *monte* when I knew my first son was dead before he lived, that either there was no god, or he was deaf to my pleas and my pain. "If it's that important to you," I said. My heart beat strongly enough to burst out of my chest.

The act itself was over before I knew it. The *mohel* did his job. My brother managed it all. I stood by the window waiting for the baby's cry and the shouts of *mazel tov*, which quickly followed. The rabbi gave Stephen a small taste of wine on a linen napkin to suck on, to put him to sleep. It worked almost instantaneously.

Charlotte did a wonderful job. She and her sisters prepared food for two days before the *bris*: blintzes, noodle kugel, platters of smoked salmon with bagels and cream cheese, all types of salads, cakes, and Danish pastries. She even made my favorite, *Tajes Kolacs*, a buttery yeast cake filled with raisins and cinnamon. I had dreamed of this when we lived in Sosúa. The mostly German refugees loved their pastry, but had neither the proper oven and equipment, nor the knowledge of this Hungarian delicacy, to produce it or anything like it.

Anabela did bake for me though in the small communal village kitchen, flakey Dominican pastries filled with *guava* paste. It was nothing like Charlotte's, but the love that went into them was the same, and I saw her smile as I closed my eyes and the aroma of yeast, sugar, and butter filled my senses.

They set up a table of spirits: rye, scotch, and cherry herring, in the corner of the living room. I would have liked a little rum, but there wasn't any. What did these people know of rum? I laughed to myself.

I poured a shot of whiskey into a delicate, cut-crystal glass and walked over to the bassinette in the far corner of the room. It was decorated in white and blue lace. A small red ribbon stuck out from under the mattress. Old superstitions die hard.

Stephen was sleeping. We were alone. Everyone else was in the dining room ravaging the tables. I took a sip of the whiskey then caressed his tiny face. His skin was warm, silky, slightly damp. He slept like an angel. What a little wine could do was amazing. I was sure he felt no pain. I was hoping the whisky would do the same for me.

As I looked at him, I saw both my face and the face of my brother, my twin for whom I had named him. A pang of sadness ran through me, tightening my chest and settling there. Would these feelings of regret and loneliness, of desperate searching for the dead, never leave me? I had feared Anabela and José would abandon me when I sailed away from paradise. I was wrong. They followed me and remained with me, comforting me when other ghosts, both living and dead, tortured me.

"Sleep, *mijo*," I whispered into Stephen's ear then kissed his cheek. "I will always be here for you. We will share so much. Someday I will take you to paradise. Then it will be your decision whether to stay or not."

"Max." It was Helen. Charlotte and Harriet were with her. "What are you doing?"

"Admiring our perfect work."

Helen walked the few steps between us gingerly, Charlotte and Harriet on either side to steady her. "Spend some time with our guests," she said. "We need to attend to him." She kissed me gently on my cheek, the way I had kissed our son. "I love you," she whispered into my ear.

I did as I was told. Mostly I felt like a lost child. I wandered into the dining room, which along with the adjacent kitchen was filled with our friends and what little family we had left. They smiled, and ate, and joked. It seemed easy for them. I looked upon them as if I were in another dimension. I didn't understand their happiness. Not their happiness for us for the birth of our child, but in general. I never felt happy. I had known happiness once, for a short time. I had tried to open myself to happiness again, but it was fleeting, like the moment I had just shared with my son.

"Have you eaten something, Uncle Max?" Helen's nephew Ernie asked me, shaking me out of my stupor. The whiskey began to settle in on my empty stomach. I felt its warmth fill me, chasing away the cold that dominated me always. "No, no, I haven't," I replied.

"Come, let me make a plate for you," his wife said.

"No, that's alright. I'm not hungry."

"But you have to eat. It's your son's *bris*."

"Yes," I said. "It is."

I would eat because that's what was expected of me, despite the fact that I preferred the hunger in my heart to a full stomach. The ghosts kept coming notwithstanding the love I felt for Stephen, so innocent and pure in his crib. Istvan's face was in front of mine now, like my own face looking back at me. He smiled. "Good luck to you, my brother," he said. "A new start. I will watch over him." The alcohol seeped deeper into my mind and memories. I hadn't eaten since the night before. Another face appeared before me. This time it was of the baby we lost in the *monte* in Santo Domingo. It was my fault. I had sent Nereida home out of anger. Then Nereida's face appeared, and José, and Anabela, gloriously pregnant. I had sacrificed all of them as well for my stubbornness. For a moment, I thought I might begin to cry, but then I looked around the room and knew I had to control myself.

Ernie's wife tugged at my shirt. "Uncle Max, come sit down, eat something."

I looked into her eyes and smiled. "Thank you," I said.

"For what?" she replied. "Enjoy! It's Aunt Charlotte's noodle pudding!"

I was thanking her for rescuing me from my ghosts, but she couldn't have known that. I took a forkful of the noodle pudding. It was delicious, rich with cheese and *lekvar*, like my mother made when I was a boy. I cleared my mind and took another bite before my mother could enter my mind and take another bite out of me. I had let her die, herded like cattle into a gas chamber.

"Would you like anything else?" Ernie's wife asked.

She was forcing me to focus. "Yes, some *tajes kolacs*, please."

"Max," my brother Jack said from behind. He sat next to me and put his hand on my forearm.

"I want to tell you how happy I am for you. We all are," he said, leaning into me and whispering in my ear, "We have all been through too much, but you especially."

He didn't know how much, as I hadn't told him everything.

"This is a new start for both of you and for us. Please, don't be a stranger."

I appreciated his words. The distance that remained between us was my own fault. To be fair, he tried. I was always a little detached, unwilling to accept his affection and his help. I'm not sure that's unusual for people like us. There were resentments that were undeserved, but still there. "I won't," I said. "I promise."

He hesitated for a moment. "Charlotte and I were talking. The tenant upstairs is moving out. We thought, perhaps, you and Helen would consider moving in. The commute to midtown isn't bad by subway, and we could be so much help to you."

I appreciated his offer, more than I wanted to admit to myself. There was a part of me that wanted it, that wanted to embrace the closeness he offered. I had lost my twin brother, my best friend, and so much else. I also knew what living in the same building with my brother Jack would mean. I would have to bury my resentment of his god. He lived a kind of life that I couldn't and wouldn't, in subservience to a vengeful, mocking god in whom I didn't believe. "I'll speak to Helen," I said, both of us knowing full well I would never make the move.

"Thank you," he said. He took my hand in his. "I would welcome it."

"A *mazel tov*," said a man in a dark, crumpled, suit still wearing his hat standing behind Jack. Jack turned. "Rabbi, thank you," he said. "Let me introduce you. This is my brother, Max."

"I know," said the Rabbi, in Hungarian. He had the thick, sing-song accent common to people from Budapest.

"Max, this is Rabbi Birnbaum. He's our Rabbi at the Commonwealth Avenue *Shul*."

I began to rise and offered him my hand.

"No, no, please don't get up. Rest, you're the child's father, you're going to need it." He sat his heavy frame down next to Jack.

"I'm used to little sleep," I said. "We were farmers in the Dominican Republic."

"Yes, yes, your brother told me. You escaped to that place. How fortunate you are that you and your wife were able to come here."

"My brother helped us," I said. "We've been here a few years."

"And thank *HaShem* for that. Here you can more easily live as a Jew."

I swigged down the last of my whiskey amplifying its already potent effect. The amber liquid burned as it slid down to my stomach. My rancor met it halfway. This was exactly what I didn't want. I was done with this. I had agreed to this ritual only for Helen's sake, and because of her insistence. My anger rose, uncontrollable. Jack looked at me. He knew the Rabbi had tread on quicksand. He pleaded me with his eyes to let it go.

I smiled sardonically at the Rabbi, considering whether to respond or just let this pass. In a moment I knew I couldn't. "What makes you think I couldn't live as a Jew there, or that I want to live as one here?" I said, loud enough for everyone to hear.

Jack touched my hand. "Please Max, not today, he has no idea."

The Rabbi sat in disbelief. He didn't know how to respond. He would have been wise to have excused himself and left, but people judge you by who and what they think you are, not who you really are. He'd made assumptions. He should have learned who I was, first.

I rose from the table and looked down at the Rabbi still seated, his face reddening. "I have no desire to live as a Jew, here or anywhere," I said. "Why would I honor a god who has stolen so much from me. And as to here versus there, at least there, a man is smart enough to learn something about the person to whom he speaks before he speaks, rather than to assume he already knows who that man is, and what he believes."

❧❧❧

Karin closed the diary and placed it on the coffee table. "Wow. Is that how you feel, Tol?"

"Sometimes."

She took his hand and placed it on her stomach. The baby moved gently under his fingers. "I've tried to talk about this with you so many times. You close down."

Tolya let out his breath slowly. "It's hard to talk about, and it's always a little strange reading Max's words. I think there's this connection, no it's more like a reflection of my life in his. He's driven by two things, his disappointment with this Jewish thing and…" He stopped and took his hand from Karin's stomach.

"Go on."

Tolya took a deep breath. Karin knew he was overwhelmed by his emotions. This was the point where he always closed down. "Please Tolya, I love you, please, just say it."

The tears were visible along the rims of his eyes. "It's the twin thing. Only a twin understands what it's like to lose their twin. He gets it. We may be separated by nearly fifty years, and we've never known each other, but we have had the same experience." Tolya held his composure as a tear escaped his eye, trailing slowly down his cheek.

"Not a day goes by that I don't think of Oleg. And I blame my father and his Jewish thing for losing him."

Then the sobs came quickly, having been held inside for so long. Karin took Tolya in her arms and cradled him against her breasts. "Shhh, *mi amor*, go ahead, it's time to feel it. It's been there too long."

Chapter 12
Washington Heights, NYC
6 August 2008
9:30 a.m.

Tolya smiled to himself as Miriam Rivera sauntered into the station. She wore a floral sun dress and a huge floppy hat; the kind of outfit Marilyn Monroe might have worn for a stroll on a boardwalk in a 1950's comedy.

"*Hola*, detective," she said waving. "I am so happy maybe you find my Nando's killer?"

Tolya waved back. "Come this way," he said, ushering her toward the rear of the precinct.

Pete was already waiting in the interrogation room. He had turned up the temperature a bit on the air conditioning. The room was too cold. He stifled a chuckle when he saw Miriam Rivera's latest outfit. She was clearly enjoying her unexpected, third, fifteen-minutes-of-fame. "Thanks for coming over on such short notice," Pete said.

"Oh, is nothing," Rivera said, removing her hat and fixing her hair. "I wait too much years for this."

"Please, have a seat," Tolya said.

Miriam walked around the table to the far end. She lowered herself gently into the seat, crossing her legs as if she were sitting side-saddle on a horse.

"Would you like something to drink before we get started?" Pete asked.

"Sure."

Pete pointed to the cans of soda on the table in the corner of the room.

Miriam frowned. "Actually, is a little cold in here. *Tenía un cafecito?*"

"*Por supuesto.* How do you take that?"

"Black with three sugar."

Pete picked up the phone and punched in the extension for the front desk. "Could you bring in a coffee please? Black with three sugars," he repeated. A few moments later the duty officer appeared, Styrofoam cup in hand. Miriam Rivera smiled and took a sip then made a face.

Tolya scribbled on the upper margin of his pad waiting for Miriam to drink her coffee. "Can we start?"

"Of course," replied Miriam. "So, you find the person who killed my Nando?"

Tolya smiled. "We're making some progress. We wanted to talk to you about the relationship between Nando and the men who owned the rooming house."

"You think they kill him?"

"I didn't say that."

"I always think they have something to do with it."

"Why?" Pete asked.

"Because who else was there?"

"It's possible he had enemies," Pete said.

"No, everybody love Nando. No enemies."

"Ms. Rivera...,"

"Miriam…"

I mean Miriam, could you tell us what kind of relationship Nando had with Ernesto Eisen and Máximo Rothman."

Miriam chuckled. "You know is so many year, I forgot their names. *Sí,* Ernesto *y* Máximo. They were friends. You know they go out with the other Dominicano*s* to the night clubs. We went a lot to those clubs in those days." Rivera raised her chin and smiled, remembering her youth.

"You went with them?" Tolya asked.

"Sometime."

"Did you know their wives?"

"*Sí,* one was Ava, Ernesto's wife, she work with him at the rooming house, so I know her better, and the other was," she furrowed her brow, tapping her head gently with her index finger, "let me remember…"

"Helen," said Tolya.

Miriam smiled and straightened her back. "*Sí, sí,* Helen. I don't know her so much. She have a son, a boy, so she stay home to take care of him. But I remember her, very nice, very quiet."

"So, you didn't see their wives much?"

"No."

"What did Ava do at the rooming house?"

"She do the cooking and some cleaning. She were a very good cook. I remember. Sometime I eat there with them there. If I was there, she would invite me to stay. She cook Dominican food like she were born there."

Pete had to suppress his smile again. "She knew how to cook platanos?"

Miriam laughed knowingly. She nearly spilled her coffee. "No so much, platanos," she said. "In those days was hard to get. Other things. She cook in the way Dominican people cook, everything in the pot and lots of rice with beans."

Miriam took a pack of Virginia Slims and a lighter from her bag and placed it on the table. She placed one cigarette between her lips and held it there, waiting for Pete or Tolya to light it.

"I'm sorry, *señora*," said Tolya. "No smoking in here. Department rules."

She put the cigarette back in the pack then looked at the nearly empty coffee cup.

"Would you like more coffee?" asked Pete.

"No. Is no very good."

Tolya glanced at his pad looking for the next question. "You said Ernesto's wife did some of the cleaning. Who else cleaned? Did anyone else work there?"

"Sometime the other wife..."

"Helen, Máximo's wife."

"Yes, Helen, she come to do some cleaning. No one else work there regular though. Except the boy came to do some chores. He was maybe twelve-year-old and very shy."

"What kind of chores?"

"He would take out the garbage from the rooms and the kitchen and he would take the garbage pails out to the curb when the city come to pick it up. You could see he didn't like to be there."

"What do you mean?'

"He were how you say, *incomodo*."

"Uncomfortable." Pete translated. "In what way?"

"Well you know sometimes when he would come by to do his things, his father and the other guy they would be standing on the street talking with women and I think this make the boy feel a little embarrass."

"Did this happen a lot?" Tolya asked?

"It depend. When the weather was nice, Máximo and Ernesto they would sit outside and talk to the neighbors and the people from the neighborhood and sometimes they would flirt with the women. You know how that is."

Tolya glanced at Pete. "Well, that aside, let's get back to Nando and his relationship with the owners. Did they ever fight?"

"What you mean, like with these?" Miriam balled her fists and held them up. "Like this?" she said, jabbing her fists in the air.

Tolya leaned back in the chair. "No, did they ever argue?"

"About what?"

"Anything"

Miriam thought for a moment. "No really, but there was one thing."

"What was that?"

"They was always saying that he look like someone they know from Santo Domingo and he always say no, that not him."

"Can you tell us a little more about that?" Pete said. He leaned forward a bit over the table and flashed a seductive smile at Miriam. She responded in kind, a girlish giggle following.

"*Entonces*, it was like this. Nando was from the Capital."

"How do you know that?"

"Because he told me. He not gonna lie to me. And beside sometimes we would send money to his brother in Santo Domingo and I would go with him to the Western Union to send the money and I remember I help him to make out the papers for the address and it was in the city of Santo Domingo. Anyway, Ernesto and Máximo, they was from the *Cibao*, near Puerto Plata and all the time they would say, Nando, you sure you no a *Cibaeno*?

"A *Cibaeno* is someone from the *Cibao*, the northern part of the country on the Atlantic side," explained Pete. Sosúa is near Puerto Plata, on the Atlantic, in the *Cibao*."

"*Sí, sí*, that's right!" Rivera nodded her head vigorously," they from Sosúa, Judios de Sosúa."

Tolya knew what that meant without translation.

"I remember he would get very *molestada* when they said this."

Tolya looked at Pete.

"Irritated."

"Why?"

"I don't know."

"One time he got so angry he grab Máximo by the arm and tell him if he say this again he gonna make him sorry."

"What did Máximo do?"

"He grab him back and I think they gonna have a fight." She balled her fists up again for emphasis. "Ernesto has to separate them."

"Was Nando closer with Máximo or Ernesto?" Pete asked.

Miriam thought for a moment. "He wasn't close with either one, but he was more *comodo* with Ernesto. Máximo was always a little cold to him, like he didn't like to have him around."

"But you said they were friends," Tolya said.

"You know how those things go. They go out together, they hang around at the same place, they behave like all men do, but they weren't really friend. They came from the same world. They were *conocido*."

Tolya looked at Pete again.

"Like, acquaintances."

"Did you ever hear them fight about money, or the rent?"

"No, never."

"You're sure about this? Nando wasn't behind in his rent?"

Miriam made a face. "Never."

"How do you know?"

"Because every week he give me the money to go to the bank to buy a money order for the rent. He want to have a receipt so he can always show that he pay the rent."

Tolya glanced at Pete again, raising his left eyebrow slightly. Pete nodded back almost imperceptibly. It was a non-verbal code they had developed over years of interrogations, indicating that they both had enough information, that they had learned what they needed to know. "Thanks for coming in to speak with us," Tolya said. "We will let you know if we need to ask you anything else."

"That's all?" Miriam Rivera said. She seemed genuinely disappointed.

"Yes," Tolya replied.

"I hope I help you," she said, getting up from the chair and smoothing her dress. She put her hat back on and straightened it then walked around the table and offered her hand, first to Tolya and then to Pete. "Perhaps you would come for dinner when you solve the case."

"We'd be happy to," said Pete, as Miriam walked out of the interrogation room.

"I feel sorry for her," Tolya said. "She's mourned for this guy her whole life."

"Me too, she never let go. I know how that feels." Pete said, a faraway look in his eyes.

"You been there, bro? You got something we should talk about?"

"Yes. Maybe sometime, brotherman. Not now. And wow, that was a revelation."

"That's for sure. Her version of events kinda shoots Erno's whole story to pieces," Tolya said.

"But after all these years and coming from two really old people, I don't know. Questions is who's lying?"

"Who has reason to lie?" Tolya said. "Erno didn't kill this guy."

"We know that already." Pete picked up the case file from the table and leafed through it. The question is who did. And why is Erno covering for that person."

"You think it could have been Máximo? She said they didn't much get along."

"Nah," Pete said. "Why would Erno bother to lie now, to cover for him? Máximo's dead. As a matter of fact, why wouldn't he just say Máximo killed him. That would have been the end of it. You can't prosecute a dead man."

"True. If he's covering for anybody that person has to be living?"

"True. Those other two guys who reported him missing, they still alive? Can we track them down?"

"I checked that already," Pete said pulling a sheet of paper from the file with his notes in the margin. "One is dead for years, the other, no trace of him."

"Was there anything in the statements they gave that might help us?"

Pete's expression changed; his anger evident. "Tol, there weren't any statements in the file. Those two Irish cops who handled this case couldn't have cared less. Nando Vargas was one more spic, gone. They were happy to see him go. They didn't care if he was alive in Florida, or dead and dumped on Roosevelt Island."

"Are either of them alive?"

"I don't know. Why? You wanna speak with those two racists?"

"If they're alive, I think we have to."

Chapter 13
Washington Heights, NYC
7 August 2008
10:30 a.m.

Shalom looked up from the passage of Talmudic commentary he was reading when he heard the tap on his door. "Rabbi, may I come in?" came Faigl's voice, more diminutive than usual. She squeezed herself through the door before Shalom could reply.

Shalom sensed some urgency in her demeanor. As always, she averted her gaze, but this time came up to the edge of his desk. She had never come that close before. Her shoulders were hunched up, unusually tense, even for Faigl.

"Those policemen are back," she said, her hands clasped in front of her. Shalom had his answer as to her odd behavior. "Rabbi, why do they keep coming back here? Is something wrong? Has someone threatened us?" Her fear was palpable.

"No, Faigl. There's nothing wrong, and nothing to be frightened of," Shalom replied, trying to calm her. "Please, show them in."

Faigl walked silently out of the room, her head down, shoulders still up. Tolya and Pete entered Shalom's study a moment later. Shalom stood up behind his desk. "How are you, detectives? Please, have a seat." He closed the volume of Talmud on his desk. "Have you learned from Erno what you hoped to know?"

Tolya smirked as he sat down on the wood chair. He considered how much he hated being in this office. Too many memories. "Somewhat. Now we have some more questions for you."

Pete took an accordion folder from under his arm, placed it on his lap and opened it. He took a photograph from inside and placed it on the desk, watching Shalom's his face for a reaction. "Do you know this man?"

Shalom picked up the photo and stared at it. His eyes lingered on the pencil line mustache. He viewed the style as alien, something that defined the wearer as other, not American. He remembered his mother's happiness when his father shaved his, just after he sold the rooming house and went to work at a hotel in Midtown. "You look like a *gringo* now," she had said, laughing a little. "That's what you wanted," his father replied, walking out of the room. His mother sat down on their bed. She didn't know Shalom was watching from the hallway as she wiped away a tear from her eye. Those moments of his father's subtle cruelty toward his mother lingered in Shalom's memory forever.

"No, I'm afraid I don't know this man," Shalom said.

Tolya took the photo back. "Funny, we thought you would recognize him. That's Nando Vargas, the man we found in the wall of the house on 187th Street. He was one of your father's boarders."

Shalom's expression remained cordial. "My father and Erno had a lot of boarders. It was a rooming house. People came and went frequently. As I told you, I didn't spend much time there."

Tolya smiled. "That's not what we've heard."

"Detective," Shalom said, leaning forward over the desk. He had to force himself to remain affable. "What could you possibly be talking about? I was twelve years old when my father sold that business. How much time could I possibly have spent there? Honestly, I've told you all I know about this long-finished chapter in my family's history."

"We're not sure that's exactly accurate," said Pete. "We're trying to solve a case here and would appreciate your help."

"We interviewed the victim's girlfriend," Tolya said.

Shalom interrupted him, flabbergasted. "His girlfriend? Forty years later?"

"Yes," Tolya continued. "She's quite interested in helping us solve the case."

Shalom found containing his irritation difficult. He recalled the disdain with which Kurchenko spoke to him the night his father was found unconscious. He had a penchant for the dramatic, this detective, but Shalom would maintain his composure. *HaShem* was with him. "What did she say, and what does that have to do with me?"

"She remembers you quite clearly. She says you were at the rooming house frequently. Chores, helping out."

Shalom continued to suppress his growing anger. It occurred to him that Kurchenko had a unique ability to get under his skin. He wasn't going to give the detective the pleasure he sought, to see Shalom unnerved. "Yes, I helped out." Shalom chuckled masking his irritation. "I was my father's only son. He needed help. I emptied the garbage and pulled the trash out to the curb three times a week."

Tolya held up the 8 x 10 glossy again. "But you don't recognize this man?"

"No, I don't. I told you. My father had many boarders. I steered clear of them as much as I could. They were never a very happy, or pleasant bunch. What kind of people do you think rent rooms in a boarding house anyway, detective?"

Tolya sensed Shalom's control beginning to break. He handed the photo back to Pete who returned it to the file. This was a good point to ratchet things down. "Thank you, Rabbi. Sorry to have bothered you." Pete picked up his signal to leave.

Shalom pressed a button on his desk phone. A moment later Faigl entered the room. "Faigl will see you out. Please, let me know if there is anything else I can help you with. I hope you find your murderer." At the word murderer, Shalom saw the color drain from Faigl's face. He opened the volume of Talmud still on his desk, breathing in more deeply than he normally would, beseeching the words on the page to offer him the peace he found only in its passages.

Shalom exhaled slowly after Kurchenko and Gonzalvez left the room. What difference did any of this make? It was so long ago. Nearly forty years. He recalled his childhood almost as if it were a story being told to him by someone else. But the pain of that time came rushing back every time Kurchenko came to see him, truthfully, every time he gazed across the rooftop of the Buszek School to the wood frame house on 187th Street. He would welcome its departure from his view and his life. He closed his eyes and breathed deeply again. He wanted to forget, he needed to forget but, he wasn't sure he could.

Washington Heights, NYC
June 1966

"Istvan," his father called out waving to him. "Hurry up, we have a lot to do today."

He hated when his father addressed him in Hungarian, especially in the street. His name was Stephen, not Istvan. He wanted to be like other kids, with American parents who spoke English the right way, no accent.

"I'm coming, father," he called back in English as he trudged up the hill.

Stephen spoke Hungarian just fine, well enough to understand everything he heard his parents say in hushed tones when they didn't want him to understand, but he wasn't going to speak it, at least not in the middle of the street. Who knew who might be around, one of his classmates, or the other kids from the neighborhood?

"You're late," his father said pointing to his watch. "I asked you to be here half an hour ago."

"I'm sorry father. I had a lot of homework," Stephen lied. The school year was nearly over, and he had little to do. He just didn't want to do this. He didn't understand why he was needed to help paint the room for the new boarder. His father had said it was time for him to begin to learn how to do things they didn't teach in school.

Max smiled. "Okay. I suppose that comes first. Is your mother home yet?"

"Yes," she said we should be home by six thirty for dinner.

"Ah, he's arrived," came a shout from the window on the third floor. "It was Uncle Erno, his father's best friend. The friend he called brother, though Stephen knew his only real uncle was Uncle Jack who lived in the Bronx. All his other uncles and aunts, along with his grandparents and cousins had died in Europe. The Nazis had killed them. Erno, his father had told him on many occasions, was his brother-in-life. He, unlike Uncle Jack, had lived through what his father had. Only Erno understood the events that had shaped Max.

Max shouted back, "*Sí, ya subimos.*"

Despite his momentary anger with his father, Stephen was amazed, as always, by the way he could switch between languages in the tiniest of moments. He almost always spoke Spanish with Uncle Erno, and with people in the neighborhood from time to time. At home it was Hungarian with his mother, in the street it was English, unless the person to whom he was speaking was Hungarian or Spanish. He was many things Max Rothman, Hungarian, Dominican, occasionally Jewish and always charming, a trait that dazzled his son.

"Come, up we go," Max said.

Stephen followed his father up the three flights to the top floor of the rooming house. The room they were about to paint had been empty for several months. Uncle Erno and his father had removed all the furniture from the room, save the metal bed frame. The furniture, a large wooden closet, a dresser, two chairs, a small table, and the mattress lined the third-floor hall.

"*Szervusz*," Uncle Erno greeted him in Hungarian. "Come give your Uncle a big hug.

Stephen loved Uncle Erno. He was always happy and had lots of interesting stories. He said he was a communist before the war, a rich communist. Stephen didn't really understand how anyone could be rich and a communist at the same time. He would never mention to anyone that Erno was a communist. He knew that was something people didn't like. Stephen hugged Erno tightly. He smelled of paint and sweat.

"I see you got started," said Max.

"Yes, I figured I should. It has to dry by tomorrow, when he arrives."

Max smirked and nodded his head. "Yes, he arrives tomorrow. He gave you the first two weeks?"

"The girlfriend gave me the money yesterday. She asked if we would take money orders in the future instead of cash."

"What did you tell her?"

"I told her money orders were all right. No checks."

"Good."

Stephen had no idea what they were talking about, regardless of the language they would have used. He didn't know what a money order was. "What should I do?" he asked.

"Put these on," Max said tossing him a white T-shirt and a pair of gloves.

The T-shirt was his father's. It hung on him like a dress. "Papa, it's too big."

"It will protect your clothes." Max unbuttoned his own shirt and hung it over the banister in the hallway, a sleeveless T-shirt exposing his arms and shoulders. "Like the old days, no?" he said to Erno.

"*Sí*, you remember those times? You had no clue how to dress for manual labor."

"And you did?"

They laughed.

Stephen tried on the gloves. They were a bit loose, but he thought he could manage with them. "Are these too big too?" Stephen asked, holding up his hands.

Max frowned. "Take those off as well. You won't be able to hold the brush properly."

"Well, I tried," said Erno. "We have plenty of turpentine."

"Okay, my American boy," said Max, his tone warm and gentle. "Let's learn how to paint." Max picked up a small brush and handed it to Stephen. "You hold it like this."

He placed the handle of the brush flat into his palm. "You dip the brush into the paint in this tray. Nice and slow and even. You let the paint soak in a little then you run the brush against the edge of the tray to remove the excess, so it doesn't drip." Max demonstrated, wiping the excess paint off the edges of the brush gently and purposefully. "You see?" he said, shifting his gaze from the paint brush to Stephen.

"Yes, father." Stephen repeated the action as Max instructed. When he looked up, both Erno and his father were smiling.

"*Nagyon jol*," Erno said in Hungarian, "very good."

Stephen smiled. As much as he became impatient and sometimes embarrassed by his father and uncle, especially when they were together, and especially if they had had something to drink, he loved them both, and it pleased him when he did something, anything, that made them happy.

"Now, you see those areas between where Uncle Erno has painted the wall with the roller and the molding along the bottom?"

"Yes," Stephen replied.

"That's what you're going to paint. Like this."

Max took the brush from Stephen's hand and gently glided it along the wall. The smell of the paint was strong. Stephen looked at his right hand. Some paint had gotten onto it. He wiped it against his T-shirt, but that only smeared it more.

"Don't worry about that, we will clean you up later," said Erno.

"Here," Max said, handing Stephen the brush, adding yet more wet paint to Stephen's hand.

Max grabbed one of two paint rollers on extension sticks. 'Uncle Erno and I will roll out the other three walls and then you will do the same to these, fill in where we can't reach with the roller."

Stephen nodded. He knelt down and gently brushed the paint onto the plaster surface of the wall. The edge of his T-Shirt caught under his knees. He nearly fell over as he tried to move forward. Regaining his balance, he took a few more brushes against the old, dirty paint, the smudges and discoloration disappearing under the new, fresh, coat. The result of his efforts gave him the same satisfaction he got from a good grade at school. "Is this okay?" he asked.

"That's perfect," Max said.

"Where did you learn to paint, papa?"

"In Sosúa," replied Max.

"Your father was something of an aristocrat in those days," Erno said, pushing the roller up against the wall opposite Stephen. The spray from the roller misted onto Erno's face and hair, leaving tiny droplets.

"What your uncle means is that I had no idea how to paint…"

"Or do much of anything else," interrupted Erno.

"Oh, and you did?"

"No," Erno said, laughing again.

"So how did you learn?" Stephen asked, covering the smudges on the dirty, old wall with his brush.

Max pulled and pushed his roller across the corner wall, up and down in even strokes. "We needed to paint the new concert hall at the settlement. Naturally, we had to do it ourselves."

"Then José showed up and he did more in one hour than we did in half a day," Erno interjected.

"That was always the case," said Max.

"Who is José?" Stephen asked.

Max hesitated. "He was my friend, my best friend."

Stephen was confused. "I thought Uncle Erno is your best friend."

"You can have more than one best friend," Uncle Erno replied.

"Where is José now?" Stephen asked.

There was a long moment of silence before Erno answered. "He died in Santo Domingo."

Stephen knew instinctively not to ask for details.

"And soon he will rest in peace," Max mumbled.

Stephen turned back to the wall and covered the rest of the old paint with the new. He wished he could do something like that for his father sometime, to cover his old, dark memories with something new and bright, the way he brushed away the smudges on the wall.

The following afternoon Stephen was back at the rooming house to empty the trash from the rooms and to haul it out to the street for pick-up the next morning. The furniture was back in the room on the third floor. The walls were gleaming white, but despite the open windows and the strong, warm, breeze coming through them, the room still smelled of paint and turpentine.

He carried the garbage from the third-floor bathroom down the stairs. He found his father and uncle standing in the parlor chatting with the new boarder. The man was tall and thin, and dressed in a yellow suit with a black shirt, open at the collar. He wore the kind of hat that his father and uncle wore when they went out in the evening without his mother and Aunt Ava.

"Stephen," his father said. "This is Fernando Vargas. This is my son, Stephen."

The man turned toward him and stuck out his hand. He addressed Stephen in Spanish. "*Mucho gusto, varron.*"

"He doesn't understand a word," Max said.

Stephen understood everything. He just preferred to speak English.

"The son of a Dominican, and he doesn't speak Spanish?"

"He's an American. He doesn't need to."

"Nice to meet you," the man said with an accent much heavier than his father's or uncle's. He wore a thin mustache, similar to theirs.

Stephen shook the man's hand. The man squeezed a bit too hard and it hurt. "Nice to meet you too," he said.

Chapter 14
Washington Heights, NYC
7 August 2008
12:30 p.m.

Pete parked the car in an illegal spot in front of Amsterdam House, a retirement home on Amsterdam Avenue and West 115th Street. He reached behind him to the floor under his seat and pulled out his NYPD identification card. He looked directly at Tolya, exasperated at the fact that he had agreed to come here to see the officer who had closed the case. "You really think this guy is gonna have any information, you think he's gonna remember shit? He's in an Alzheimer's facility!" he shouted tossing the ID card onto the dashboard.

"Humor me. We gotta follow every lead." Tolya stepped out of the passenger seat and checked his gun in its holster before closing the car door. The intense heat and humidity of the past week had finally broken. The weather was clear and crisp, that kind of mid-August day that he waited for every year, that jogged his memory of his boyhood summers in Ukraine Tolya laughed to himself and felt a pang of sadness at the same time. Pete was so much like Tolya's twin brother Oleg, stubborn and easily irritated, but in the end reasonable and almost surgically focused. On days like this he missed Oleg more than usual, but was glad to have Pete, more than just a substitute.

"Okay," Pete said, deferring to Tolya despite his reservations. "Let's do this. But I'm telling you right now, if he calls Vargas a spic or anything else like that, I'm gonna slug him."

A blast of air-conditioning hit them as the doors opened to the lobby of the nursing home. They approached the concierge desk, their badges in hand.

"May I help you?" asked the uniformed attendant. She wasn't much younger than the population she was serving.

"Yes, thanks," Tolya said. "We would like to see Mike O'Connor."

"We have three here, which one?"

"The former cop," Pete said.

"Ah, yes, that one." The attendant raised her eyebrow. "Let me see where he might be right now." She browsed her computer screen, picked up the phone, and punched in three numbers. "Is Detective O'Connor in the dining room? Oh, Okay, Thanks." She smiled a little too cheerily. "He's just finished lunch and is on the way to the garden. I could phone back there and let them know you want to see him."

"That would be fine," Tolya replied.

The attendant picked up the phone again, this time calling the garden. "He's there. Just arrived," she said to Tolya and Pete. "You'll find him under the maple tree at the back. His caregiver is with him. Right that way." She pointed to the long hallway to the right.

"Thanks," Tolya said. He felt Pete's hand on his shoulder holding him back.

"One minute, bro. Umm, I don't want to be indelicate," Pete said to the attendant, "but this Detective O'Connor, is he, let's say, mentally there?"

The attendant smiled. "For the most part yes, and I should warn you, very feisty."

They found O'Connor under the maple tree at the rear of the garden, exactly as the attendant had told them. He was seated in his wheelchair in blue pajamas, eyes closed. He had a head of thick, white hair, his ruddy complexion made even more red by the contrast. The old detective's attendant, a thin, dark-skinned man with a shaved head, sat on a bench next to him, reading the paper.

"Excuse me," Tolya said.

O'Connor opened his eyes. They were ice blue and animated, despite his age. "Whaddaya want?" he said, his old-fashioned Woodside accent thick and caricature-like.

Tolya flashed his badge. "I'm Detective Kurchenko and this is my partner Detective Gonzalvez."

O'Connor squinted against the intersection of shade and sunlight that obscured Pete and Tolya's faces. "Boy, the Department's changed."

Pete tapped Tolya's arm. "That's strike one."

"What you boys want?" O'Connor croaked.

"May we sit down?" Tolya asked.

"Sure," he pointed to the bench where his attendant was sitting, still reading the paper. "You wanna let these guys sit down, Franky? You can take the paper over there." He pointed toward another bench a few feet away, in the sun. "We wanna talk private."

The attendant left without a word. He crossed the garden to a bench under a smaller tree and struck up a conversation with an attractive young woman in a uniform, the attendant for an old woman who sat sleeping in her wheelchair. The sun baked the old woman like an iguana on a rock by the sea.

"What kinda name is that?" O'Connor said to Tolya. "What you say it was?"

"Strike two," Pete said.

"Kurchenko. It's Ukrainian. I'm from Russia," Tolya said in his thickest Russian accent, betraying his constant attempt to control his now almost unnoticeable foreign intonation.

"Yeah, I can tell, that's some accent you got. In my day, the force was all Americans."

"We are Americans," Pete mumbled. Tolya shot him a glance. Pete took a couple steps back into the shadows.

"You worked on a missing persons case in 1966," Tolya continued. "It's come back to us as a cold case. The body was found last week."

"That's more than 40 years ago." O'Connor said with some surprise. "I worked a lot of cases. You really expect me to remember anything about that? You see where I am? Where I'm living?"

Pete pulled the photo of Vargas from the file he was holding on his lap. He handed it to O'Connor. "You ever see this photo?"

O'Connor stared at it. He held it out to the farthest extent of his arm would reach then pulled it close to his face. "I don't know. Tell me about the case, maybe that'll jog my memory."

"He disappeared around July Fourth, nineteen-sixty-six. He was living in a rooming house on West 187th Street."

"Would you like to see the statement you and your partner made?" Pete asked, stepping out of the shadow, challenging O'Connor.

"Don't bother, I don't have my glasses here. I think I do remember this. He had a girlfriend. A real hot portorican."

"Yes, he did," said Tolya.

"She kept coming around. We thought she must be hot for me and my partner."

Tolya sensed Pete moving. He reached back with his hand and grabbed Pete's forearm. Pete moved back toward a bench near the maple tree and sat down.

"Why would you think that?" Tolya said, crouching in front of O'Connor.

"Come on, boys." The old cop chuckled. "You know how those broads are, those Spanish broads. When one man disappears, they start looking for another. What would she care anyway about this guy? He was nobody. Maybe she figured she could make something from the two of us."

Pete got up from the bench. "Where's the men's room?" he asked.

O'Connor pointed toward his attendant. "Go ask Franky."

"Can't you wait with that a few minutes, bro?" Tolya said.

"No brother, I feel like I'm gonna explode and after what we just digested, you should too."

Tolya nodded. "I do and I understand. I'll finish up here." He swallowed hard as Pete walked away. "Detective O'Connor," he continued, "Can you tell me what you remember about this case. Do you remember either of these men?" Tolya showed O'Connor the photograph of Max and Erno in front of the house on West 187th Street.

O'Connor repeated the same process he had done with the first photo. "Yeah, they owned the place. Two Jews."

Tolya tensed up. That's what this old man remembered? He was beginning to think Pete was right, this guy was too bigoted to offer any useful insight. He decided to give it one more try. "Did you interview them?"

"Yeah, mostly they were upset about the money they said he owed them. But that makes sense, they were Jews."

Tolya stifled his own revulsion of this old man. He just needed to get the information. "Do you remember anything odd about the case?"

O'Connor thought for moment. "There wasn't really anything strange or different about it. People ran out on rooming houses all the time. They didn't have the money to pay, so they just left in the middle of the night."

O'Connor seemed to lose focus, to drift off for a moment. Tolya wasn't sure he had anywhere else to go with this. He closed the file when suddenly the old man sprang back to life. "There was one thing though that just didn't make much sense," he said. "It bothered me all the way back then."

"Which is what?"

"The guy left a note. But the note was in English. He said he was going to Florida with his girlfriend to start over. Only he didn't take the girlfriend and the note was in English. The girlfriend told us he couldn't speak much English, let alone write it."

Tolya swallowed hard. How had both he and Pete missed that?

ɔɔɔ

Tolya found Pete in the car, the seat back, his eyes closed. La Mega was blasting on the radio. Tolya turned down the volume as he settled into the passenger's seat.

Pete looked at him. "Whaddaya doing? I was relaxing. He made me tense. You finished with that old, piece of shit, racist, waste-of-time?"

"Yeah, but it wasn't a waste of time."

Pete sprang up in his seat. "What the fuck you talkin' about?"

Tolya pulled the note from the file and handed it to Pete. "Look that over and tell me what's wrong with that picture."

Pete read the note over twice. "No fucking idea. You tell me."

"It's in English. Vargas didn't speak much English and couldn't write in English. Remember what Miriam Rivera told us? She did his banking and filled out all his forms and addressed his letters."

Pete's mouth opened. "Shit, how did we miss that?"

"I don't know. Shit happens. Look at the handwriting."

"*Coño*, yeah, I never would have thought about that." Pete slapped his forehead. "We have writing samples, the diaries. Let's go back to the precinct, fast." He turned the key in the ignition and began pulling out of the spot. "I'll contact the handwriting guy." Pete bumped his fist to Tolya's. "Damn brotherman, good work."

Chapter 15

Washington Heights, NYC
7 August 2008
8:30 p.m.

Karin placed the tray on the glass coffee table while sliding into the corner of the black leather couch. "Looks like you're having a little trouble maneuvering there, *amor*," said Pete.

Karin looked at him and smirked. "No cookies for you," she said, then grabbed the plate from the tray, but Pete was too quick. He nabbed two cookies with his thumb and forefinger before Karin could pull the plate out of reach. "After four kids, I'd think you'd be a little more understanding."

Pete smiled. "It was only three pregnancies. I was very attentive with the first one, but after that…well."

Karin threw a small pillow at Pete. He caught it deftly with his free hand, the cookies still in the other. "Your friend is the same way," she said, nodding in the direction of the hallway leading to the bedrooms. "With Max he was like, honey this, and, oh I'll get that for you, darling…"

Pete laughed. "I don't know how any woman puts up with either of us."

Tolya came into the living room and put the diaries down on the glass table. "I heard that." He bowed to Karin. "May I pour you a cup, dear?"

"Oh, sure." Karin rolled her eyes and reached over to take the mug from Tolya then sipped at the warm, rich, liquid. "I make pretty good coffee," she said.

"That you do," said Pete, sipping his. "And these chocolate chip cookies are pretty good too."

Tolya sat down next to Karin. He took her leg and put it over his, massaging her foot. She laughed. "Right, now that Pete is here, you're the perfect pregnancy husband."

He smiled that big Russian smile that melted her every time. "I'm trying."

"Yep," Karin said, swatting Tolya away playfully. She pulled back her leg. "Is Max asleep?"

"Off in dreamland."

Pete took one of the diaries off the coffee table and thumbed through the pages. "Did Tolya tell you about the old racist cop we saw today?"

"He mentioned it."

Pete looked at Tolya and smiled. "Did he tell you how he cracked an important fact about the case?"

Karin took Tolya's hand in hers. "No. What did you figure out? And when did you get to be so modest?"

Tolya smiled. "Let's not jump the gun. Let's see what the handwriting guy says first."

Karin glanced from Tolya to Pete and back again. "Handwriting specialist? Are one of you going to tell me?"

Pete smiled. "This old blood hound over here realized we have a handwritten note, supposedly from the victim. Problem is the note is in English and the victim couldn't write in English according to his girlfriend." Pete picked up the diary he was thumbing through earlier and held it up to Karin. "The writing looks a lot like this."

Karin's eyes widened. "You think what?"

"We think Max might have been involved. Very involved."

"Okay, then," Karin said, "we'd better get started and see what we find in there. I wanna get to sleep tonight and you know in my condition..." She patted her belly.

"Pete," Tolya asked, "what did you determine from the journals you looked at?"

"There's not much there," Pete said. "They're all from the early 50's. They alternate back and forth between Spanish and English. He switches to English when he wants to make more of an effort to move forward, forget the past. It's mostly about how unhappy he was. He feels displaced, again. He wants to go back to Santo Domingo but can't. Also, as his English improves, he uses it more. I haven't read through any of them completely yet, though. Just pieces, passages, entries."

"Interesting," said Tolya. "What I discovered was that his entries drop off after Shalom's birth. They seem to have a happier tone for a while, too. Then in this volume here, about a quarter of the way in, he begins writing in Spanish again. And he's writing a lot more."

"Which is why we're here, Pete," said Karin, nibbling at a cookie, "so we can translate."

"What year is that volume?" asked Pete.

"Nineteen-sixty-six."

"The year Vargas was murdered."

"Exactly."

Washington Heights, NYC
April 1966

I didn't believe it at first when Erno told me. I couldn't believe it was possible. I told him he was crazy. It's been over twenty years. How could he recognize him? He said no, he would never forget his face. How could he forget the man who had nearly killed me?

It seemed like another lifetime now. Erno and some of the other settlers had found me nearly dead the day after we were attacked by Trujillo's men in front of José's house. José and Nereida were dead. Anabela was missing. Erno went to the police station to inquire about her. At first, they looked at him like he was speaking Chinese. Then he pressed the duty clerk, who brought out the lieutenant commandant. He was tall and thin and very full of himself. He had no idea where Señorita Pabon might be. How would he know? When Erno described him to me I knew he was the man who had killed José and Nereida and nearly killed me. What had he done with Anabela?

I begged Erno to leave it alone, but he wouldn't. I was scared, terrified. Trujillo's men knew no limits. They could come back and finish me off if they wanted. Perhaps that would have been the best thing. But, the angry young, communist from his youth had wakened in Erno's mind. The young man who would stand up to authority even if it landed him in jail wouldn't let it go. I suppose that's what I admire about him most, his personal loyalty.

Erno returned to the police station several times more. Each time he got the same contemptuous treatment from the lieutenant, Vicente Tejada. Tejada scowled at him, mocked him as he had me that night in front of José's house. Tejada reminded Erno that he was a guest of el Jefe, Generalissimo Rafael Trujillo. This was not Erno's country. He could be deported. Erno demanded to see the lieutenant's superior officer. He told the captain that we had witnesses that put the lieutenant at the scene.

"Who could those witnesses be?" the captain pressed Erno. Finally, Erno revealed that I had survived, that I could identify my assailant. A few days later an officer of the DORSA, the agency that had established Sosúa, came to see me and Erno. He had received a visit from a representative of the government. It would be better if we dropped this incitement. I must be mistaken. Obviously, the attack had been perpetrated by criminals looking for something to steal.

Something to steal? I laughed out loud. José and Nereida, Anabela, they had nothing to steal, they had nothing at all. They didn't even have screens on their windows to keep out the mosquitos.

Trujillo's man suggested that perhaps the thieves had kidnapped Señorita Pabon. When we received a ransom note the police would search for her. Meanwhile, the lieutenant we accused of nearly murdering me was transferred elsewhere. The incident was never investigated. Anabela was gone forever, disappeared, like so many others. Eventually, I learned to accept what had happened. What choice did I have? Until now.

"Where did you see him?" I asked Erno.

"Shh, lower your voice," Erno said. "I don't want Ava to know anything about this. Or Helen for that matter."

Erno was right. It was better if Helen knew nothing about this. I wasn't sure our marriage could survive another injection of the past. And if Ava knew, Helen would know soon thereafter. "True," I said.

We were sitting in the parlor of the boarding house having a coffee. Ava was in the kitchen cleaning up from lunch. I leaned in closer to Erno on the gray velvet couch. The springs squeaked as I shifted my weight from the corner to the center.

"The first time I saw him was on Saint Nicholas Avenue, last Sunday," said Erno. "He was walking with a woman. Very pretty. They were holding hands. I followed them to the supermarket. I waited a moment then went inside. I wanted to get a better look."

"Did you?"

"Yes, pretty much. I got as close as I could. He's older than I remember, but then more than twenty years have passed, but yes, I'm sure."

"How can you be sure?"

"Some things are imprinted on us forever. His superior expression will never erase itself from my mind."

I accepted what he said. I couldn't say the same for myself. The terror of that desperate evening was a blur in my mind that would never clear, but I remembered the face of my assailant and his expression of bloodlust clearly. "When was the second time?"

"Yesterday, in the bank. I spotted him with his woman again. I got behind them in line. I heard them speaking. I recognized his voice."

"Did you follow them afterward?"

"No. But I did hear him say that he wanted to go to Las Palmas on Friday night to hear the merengue bands."

"All right then," I said. "I guess we'll be going to Las Palmas Friday night. I have to see this for myself."

"What are the two of you plotting?" said Ava, seeing us huddled together like criminals. She entered with a tray of pastries covered in wax paper which she set down on the credenza against the opposite wall.

"We're going to Las Palmas, *mi amor*, this Friday night," Erno said.

"All of us?"

Erno nodded almost imperceptibly. I understood what his gesture and his eyes told me.

"Yes, of course," I said.

"Fantastic, have you told Helen yet? We will need some new dresses."

"I will tell her tonight," I said. "We can dance. Just like old times."

The club was very crowded when we arrived. We waited outside for twenty minutes before we got in. You could hear the thump of the *merengue clave* through the walls of the building. Every Dominican in New York was there. Angel Viloria and his Orquestra was performing, and that was a big deal. For a moment, I felt like I was about to meet Anabela again on that warm night in Puerto Plata. But I knew all that was gone, Anabela, José, that club in Puerto Plata. They were the anchors that had made my life bearable again after the worst had happened.

When we finally entered the club, the room was warm and full of smoke. The walls were mirrored making the space look much larger than it was, and much more crowded. The tables were close together, huddled around the semi-circular edge of the polished wood dance floor. The music was pounding and the Dominicanos were dancing. No one dances merengue like a Dominicano. No-one loves merengue like a Dominicano. And that included me. The energy infused me. The rhythm enveloped me. We found a table toward the back and ordered drinks. Ava wanted to dance immediately. Erno convinced her to have a drink first. We had a reconnaissance mission to complete. Dancing would have to wait.

The waitress took our order and brought the drinks quickly. Though I hadn't seen our mark myself, my eyes scanned the semi-darkness for anyone who looked like the bastard who had left me for dead and killed my pregnant woman, my best friend, and his wife.

The crowd was well dressed, the men in light colored suits and the women in bright, shoulder-less dresses with spike heels in matching colors. That was one thing about people from Santo Domingo, they knew how to dress. I had pulled out my most flamboyant suit, a light blue seersucker I hadn't worn in years. Helen made a face. "Won't that be out of style," she said.

"Not for this crowd," I replied. I topped it off with a white Panama hat.

After the first round, Helen and Ava went to the lady's room to freshen up.

"Wait here for them, I'm going to look around," Erno said. They returned a few moments later. I continued to scan the room and watch Erno at the same time.

"Where's my husband?" Ava asked.

"He saw someone he knows, they waved, he went to say hello." A moment later he returned with another round of drinks.

"Why didn't you let the waitress take care of that," Ava said.

"I was there. I figured this would be faster," Erno said.

I raised my glass in a toast. "To our best friends."

Helen, Ava, and Erno raised theirs as well. "And to ours," Ava replied.

The Master of Ceremonies returned to the mike and announced the main act. The band came out dressed in costumes reminiscent of the Dominican flag, red, white, and blue, with *la escueda* emblazoned on their chests. Fringes decorated the arms of their silk shirts.

Erno nudged me and whispered in my ear as the band began to play. "At the bar, third seat from the left end, next to the woman in the pink dress with the flowers in her hair."

I looked through the smokey haze into the semi-darkness. I couldn't see much. "Let's dance," I said. Ava said yes before Helen could protest. We moved to the dance floor, swinging easily to the seductive beat. Despite our ten years in Sosúa, Helen had never learned to dance naturally. She tried her hardest though, and with one hand on my hip she kept the rhythm. I moved her across the dance floor nearer to the bar to get a better look. My heart began to beat faster, the idea of seeing this bastard again bringing too many forgotten images and thoughts back to my mind. I was dizzied with the idea that I might have a chance to take justice into my own hands, a justice that hadn't existed in Trujillo's fiefdom.

The music, though ear splitting, receded into my head. I kept the pace of the merengue with my feet while I stared at his face. Though I had been so sure I would recognize him, now I wasn't. The semi-darkness of the room and the nightmarish quality of my memory combined to cloud my certainty. Then he laughed and I knew for certain. I remembered that wild, self-impressed expression his face took on when he laughed at us in the clearing before he ordered his men to attack us. It was him, no doubt. It was him. It was Lieutenant Vicente Tejada.

At the end of the number the band switched to a new rhythm, Bachata, they called it. It was becoming very popular. Banned under Trujillo, it was the music of the patios and whorehouses, *la musica de amargues*, the sound of bitterness. I understood its passion.

I kept my eye on Tejada. I watched his every movement. I was more and more convinced. Every aspect of him returned to me, his face, his gestures, even the way he breathed. I became a creature casing its prey. He rose from his chair and moved slowly through the crowd in the direction of the bathroom. I excused myself and followed him a long moment later.

The bathroom attendant smiled and nodded as I approached the urinal. I stood next to Tejada, my heart pounding. I ignored him, my eyes staring straight forward at the wall, its textured wallpaper made to look like bamboo. A split second later, he turned and took the waiting towel from the attendant and approached the sink. I did the same. I turned on the water and lathered my hands.

"What do you think of the band?" I asked, my voice raised over the sound of the running water and the music seeping in through the doorway.

Tejada turned to me. He had no look of recognition. I considered that both a good thing and an insult. If I had killed a man, I knew his face would be in front of my eyes forever, but then god knows how many men he had killed. "As good as they are in Santo Domingo," he said, the gravelly sound of his voice cutting through my mind, travelling back decades to that moment when he told me he would kill me.

"You are Dominican?" I said, rinsing the last of the lather from my hands and wiping them with the towel the attendant provided.

"Yes, Fernando Vargas," Tejada said. He offered me his hand. "And you?"

"Máximo Rojas," I said.

"A pleasure to meet you," he replied. "I'm at the bar with my girlfriend. Why don't you join us for a drink?"

"I'd love to, but I'm here with my wife and our friends. We have a table. Why don't you join us?"

"Certainly," Vargas said without hesitation.

"We are at the back to the left of the band. It's less loud there, we can hear each other speak."

"Excellent."

I watched him as he left the men's room. The face was the same, the saunter was the same, the voice was the same, only the name was different. Despite that, I was sure. People changed their names all the time.

∽∾∽

"That's it," Tolya said. "The entry ends here. No discussion of what happened next. The next entry is dated the following day and is in Spanish.

"Man, that is odd. What do you think motivates him to change languages?" Pete said.

"Let me see that," Karin said. She took the thin grey leather volume from Tolya's hands and scanned the page. "Take another cookie while I look at this," she said. Both Tolya and Pete reached for the last remaining one. "You go ahead," Tolya said. He patted his stomach. "I gotta be careful about this anyway. When she gets pregnant, I get fat."

Pete broke the cookie in half. "Here, don't serve me up that bullshit, bro. I eat lunch with you every day. It's not the cookies."

They laughed. Tolya took half of the cookie from Pete and chomped off a large bite. "Maybe she'll make some more."

"Maybe," Karin said. She mouthed the words as she read the page. "I will tell you his handwriting hasn't improved since the earlier diaries, but his Spanish has. Perhaps he writes in Spanish when he wants to be more private with his thoughts or express himself more clearly. This passage is about how he feels about finding this guy or at least the possibility that Vargas is Tejada."

"You think he really was?" Pete said. "Maybe he just looked like him?"

"They certainly thought so," Karin said. "Here, let me translate some of this for you"

Karin hesitated a moment before starting. She wanted the translation to be correct in its emotion as well as its words.

"I am not sure how I feel, or how I should feel, or what I should do. It has been more than twenty years. Not one day goes by that I don't think of all of them, José, Nereida and Anabela, my beloved Anabela. I long for Anabela, for the life we might have had. I was never happier than I was those few months in the village with them. But I have a different life now. I have a wife, a child. In many ways Helen has given me more than anyone could be expected to give. But is that passion? The passion I had with Anabela? No, I can't say it is, but there have been moments when that passion was near. Could, would, Anabela have given me more? I'll never know. She was taken from me too soon.

And then there is Stephen. I can never replace him. I could never live without him. Yes, she carried my child too, but then had she lived, had we escaped, I would never have had this child, and this child is the thing that I wake for every day. This boy is my life.

Sadly, I can't say for certain that this man is Tejada. Last night I was so sure. In the harshness of the morning I'm not. It has been more than twenty years. I remember him only in a moment of terror. There are those who would say they never forget the face of their tormentor. I have heard that from every survivor. I believe that, but in the light of day and without both rum and hate, and the desire for revenge clouding my mind, I am not certain. Perhaps it's time to move on, finally. To accept everything that happened. Sixteen years ago, I took a small box of earth from José's grave. Perhaps the time has come to scatter it to the wind and finally say goodbye.

Chapter 16

Washington Heights, NYC
8 August 2008
8:30 a.m.

Pete tapped his fingers on the desk as he waited for a page to download. Vicente Tejada. What had this guy done? If, in fact. Vargas was Tejada, if he had killed Máximo's friends and his woman, if he was an agent of Trujillo, Pete needed to know.

Dominicans didn't like to talk about Trujillo, or those times. In private, some still yearned for it. There was law and order, people showed respect for authority. Others hissed when they heard his name. His rule and the culture that surrounded it were an embarrassment. As time passed fewer and fewer people, foreigners in particular, remembered Trujillo, or even knew his name. He had become a footnote in history. For most Dominicans, both here and there, that was just fine.

His mother's father had "worked" for Trujillo at the Country Club, Trujillo's private haunt in the Capitol. That didn't mean his grandfather supported Trujillo, it just meant he was considered reliable enough to be given a job, he wasn't likely to make trouble. At the same time, Trujillo and his henchmen stole away his grandfather's land piece by piece. That's how Trujillo operated. He gave you a job with one hand and took what was already yours—and had been your father's, and his father's before it—with the other. Pete needed to know.

He looked over the items on the google page. There were just too many Vicente Tejadas. He refined his search, added a time frame, 1960's and a town name, Puerto Plata and clicked search again. A moment later a new page downloaded.

The top entry was the title of a paper written by a graduate student at the CUNY Department of Dominican Studies. It was titled, "The Men Who Kept Trujillo in Power." It was written in 2006, a dissertation for a Ph.D. A portion was available on-line. A Vicente Tejada was mentioned.

Pete downloaded the PDF and began reading. It was very academic, too much so for him. He was looking for facts about a specific guy, not professorial musings about the underpinnings of fascism and quotes from long dead white guys on how it came to be. He skipped back to the table of contents. There were individual chapters by region for the entire country. There was one for Puerto Plata. He tried to scroll down to the page where that chapter began, only to find that the PDF contained only the first three chapters, a little over 40 pages, which ended just before the individual chapters dealing with specific parts of the country began.

Pete scrolled through the available chapters slowly, scanning the pages for the name. Toward the end of Chapter 2—Early Supporters and Enforcers of the Regime—he came upon it. Tejada was described as one of the most vicious of Trujillo's henchmen. He was from San Cristobal originally, Trujillo's hometown. He had known Trujillo since childhood, even worked on his ranch. Tejada was often in charge of fetching Trujillo's young rape victims and regularly used them himself afterward. Trujillo sent him, along with his family, to Puerto Plata after he was caught raping the daughter of one of his other henchmen in Santo Domingo, to protect him from the girl's father's wrath.

"You're here early," Pete nearly jumped out of the seat. He was so engrossed in what he was reading he hadn't heard Tolya come in. "*Coño*, don't do that."

"Sorry, brother. What you got there?"

Pete pointed to the screen. "Look here, Vicente Tejada. He did exist. They didn't make him up."

Tolya peered over Pete's shoulder, squinting at the screen. He needed to get some reading glasses, but he didn't want to give in to it. "The question is whether he's also Nando Vargas," Tolya mumbled.

"I think we need to contact this guy. This document is his thesis," Pete said as he googled the author. "Appears he's still at CUNY."

"Close enough. What's his name?"

"William Tejada."

"Well, that's a coincidence."

"Common enough name." Pete picked up the phone.

William Tejada's office was in a stately, old building at the center of the City University Campus in Hamilton Heights. Tejada had moved up the academic ladder in the few years since his dissertation. He was now the head of the Dominican Studies Program. Pete chuckled.

"What's funny?" asked Tolya.

"If I'd known I could major in Dominicans, maybe I would have gone to college."

"Yeah." Tolya nodded his head. "And you would have gotten straight A's," They both laughed.

"Excuse me," Pete said, addressing the woman behind the desk as he slowly opened the wood and glass door with the gold lettering. They flashed their badges. "We have an appointment with Doctor Tejada."

The receptionist appeared to be about twenty-five. With her black hair pulled back into a ponytail, she was pretty but appeared stony-faced. She finished typing whatever she was working on into her computer before acknowledging them. "And you are?" she said. Her complexion was the color of light coffee, her eyes deep and dark. Bright red lipstick covered her full lips, accentuating the high cheekbones and gleaming white teeth, the look Pete loved. He flashed his most seductive smile, the one that always got a phone number, but her expression remained cool.

"Detectives Gonzalvez and Kurchenko. I'm Gonzalvez."

"Do you have an appointment?"

"Yes, I spoke with Professor Tejada earlier. He said to come right over."

The receptionist pointed to the chairs across from her desk against the wall. "Have a seat, please." She disappeared into Tejada's office, otherwise ignoring them.

"Good looking woman," Pete said as they sat down.

"Yeah, just your type, too." Tolya looked at his watch, hesitating for a moment, playing with Pete. "Looks like you're losing your touch."

"Whaddaya mean?" Pete replied, taking a swipe at his partner's head. Tolya caught Pete's hand before it grazed him.

"You pulled out the smile. She couldn't care less," Tolya teased, knowing how sensitive Pete was about this.

"Ah, she's just playing cool." Pete crossed his arms against his chest and looked over at the receptionist's desk again.

Tolya laughed.

The receptionist came back into the room from Tejada's office, leaving the door open behind her. "The professor will see you know."

"*Gracias, mi amor,*" Pete said as they walked past her. He flashed the smile again. This time the receptionist returned it. He let Tolya pass him as they entered. "Told ya," Pete whispered.

Professor Tejada sat behind a large, oak desk. He was a young man, very thin, no more that 30 or 32, with a high forehead and a goatee. His hairline was receding. He wore tortoise shell glasses, perched on the ridge of his nose. His complexion was lighter than Pete's, a sure sign of why he was more easily accepted into the rarefied world of American academics than a darker skinned Dominican would have been. Though seated, they knew he was no more than about 5'7".

The office was bright and sunny and lined with bookshelves, some of them open and some cased in glass. All the titles along one wall were in English, along the other wall, all in Spanish.

"Thanks for seeing us on such short notice, Professor. I'm Pete Gonzalvez and this is my partner, Tolya Kurchenko."

"Please, sit down," Tejada said, gesturing to the two up-holstered, brocade chairs opposite his desk. "You said Gonzalvez not Gonzalez detective?"

"Yes."

"That's unusual. Not typically Dominican."

"No, my father's father was Brazilian. He came to Santo Domingo on a merchant ship from Brazil that was on its way to the United States around 1920. They were picking up bananas. That's when he met my grandmother. On the way back to Brazil they stopped in Santo Domingo again. Seems she was pregnant. He stayed."

"That's quite a story." Tejada laughed.

"Truth can be stranger than fiction."

"True. So, gentlemen how can I help you?"

"We are doing some research on Vicente Tejada. As I mentioned on the phone, I found a reference to him in your doctoral dissertation."

"And why are you investigating him?"

"A cold case," said Tolya.

"It must be very cold. He's been dead for over 40 years."

"Can you tell us a bit about him?"

"Of course. Perhaps first I should tell you he was my grandfather's brother."

"Ah, that accounts for the name," said Tolya.

"Yes."

"How did you become interested in him, in this sub-ject."

Tejada leaned back into his chair. He thought for a moment before answering. "I was born here, in New York. My parents immigrated from Santo Domingo a few years before I was born. They talked about Santo Domingo constantly. I visited when I was very small and then not again till I was seventeen. I had an epiphany when I was there as a teenager, I went for the summer and lived with my father's parents."

"What part of the country?' asked Pete.

"Puerto Plata."

"I'm from the Capital, myself," Pete said. "What was this revelation?"

"For the first time in my life I felt like I was home, like I belonged."

Both Pete and Tolya chuckled. "We both understand. I'm from Moscow," Tolya said.

"The immigrant's dilemma." Tejada nodded before continuing. "When I came home, I started reading more about Santo Domingo. I became interested in our history. I learned a little about Trujillo and was both shocked and ashamed by what I read. Then I started college here at CUNY. I decided to make Dominican studies my major. As I learned more about our history, I became curious about what my family's experience was under Trujillo. My parents weren't very forthcoming about it. I went back to Santo Domingo to see my grandfather again when I was 20. I asked him. He told me about his brother and his involvement with Trujillo's regime. I was horrified that we were in any way involved with this part of our history."

"So, you wrote your dissertation on it," said Pete.

"Yes, it was a way of expunging it from my psyche."

"What happened to Vicente Tejada?" asked Tolya.

"He was killed by an anti-Trujillista mob in the uprising in 1964."

Pete reached into the file he was holding on his lap. He took out the photograph of Nando Vargas and placed it on the desk in front of Tejada. "Is this Vicente Tejada?" he asked.

Tejada picked up the photo and examined it. He opened his draw and pulled out a file, taking some old photos from it. He compared them. "He is a few years older here than in the photos I have, but yes, I would say this photo is of him."

"What year did you say he died?" Tolya asked.

"Nineteen-sixty-four. I have a confirmed death certificate from Santo Domingo."

"This photograph was taken in nineteen-sixty-six," said Pete. "Here in New York."

Chapter 17

Washington Heights, NYC
8 August 2008
3:30 p.m.

S halom picked up his bag and turned off the air-conditioner. The Yeshiva could wait a few hours. He had a special activity planned with Baruch at the schoolyard across Broadway to toss around the basketball. Out of desperation and sadness he had abdicated parenting Baruch to Carlos, throwing himself into his teaching and his students. Now he would change that.

"Will you be returning, Rabbi?" Faigl asked as he closed the door.

"No," he smiled, "see you tomorrow."

Though she tried to hide it, Faigl's usual look of panic at any change in schedule or routine contorted her face. "Did you want me to call you with your messages at five-thirty?" Shalom smiled again. "No, I'm incognito for the evening," he said, walking slowly toward the stairs knowing full well that Faigl was wondering what he was up to.

Thankfully, the weather had cooled. Shalom stood at the corner of 186th street and Broadway and waited for the light to change. The BX 7 bus sailed by as the light flashed DON'T WALK. An old woman standing next to him cursed under her breath then looked up at him and blushed. "Sorry, Rabbi."

"Don't think twice about it," he replied. "They don't pay the necessary attention to passengers. Do you need any help with that?" He pointed at her shopping bags filled with groceries.

The old woman hesitated at first. As the light changed and they began to cross she said, "Yes, if you wouldn't mind. This one is quite heavy. Just to the bus stop."

Shalom took the bag and smiled. "My pleasure." They crossed the street together, the crossing light blinking red. "May I put this down here?"

"Of course," the old woman replied. "And thank you."

"You're welcome." Shalom smiled and turned. Looking at the chain link fence that separated the playground of PS 48 from the street, he wasn't sure where to enter. There was a gate in the fence about fifteen feet up Broadway, but it was padlocked. Several boys were playing at one of the basketball hoops. He considered asking them but didn't, walking instead toward 187th Street. He saw Carlos and Baruch at the corner, Carlos waving at him.

"This way," Carlos called out, pointing up 187th Street. Shalom noticed the smile on Baruch's face, that smile that had so enchanted him when Baruch was little, but which had disappeared by the time he was four. It hadn't returned till this past year or so. He embraced Baruch when he arrived at the corner. "Hello, son," he said. Baruch nodded; his expression unchanged.

"Say hello," Carlos said in a low controlled voice, smiling and looking directly at Baruch.

"Hello, papa," Baruch said, haltingly.

Shalom was taken aback every time he heard Baruch's voice. He had waited almost a lifetime to hear it. "I don't know how you do that, Carlos."

"It's easy Rabbi, it's just teaching him about love and trust."

Shalom felt himself choke up for a moment. Love and trust, the basis of his faith, yet he didn't know how to transmit those simple human emotions to his son. He looked up at the ghost houses across 187th street. His father hadn't known how either. Shalom quickly took back control over his emotions. "How do we get in?" he asked, as much to take his mind off the past, as to know where to enter.

"Over there." Carlos pointed at the front entrance gate to the school some twenty feet up from the corner. They walked together up the hill. Shalom looked across the street at the now silent construction site. He was both sad and glad the old house was nearly gone. It was time to move on.

Now in the schoolyard, Shalom removed his tie and jacket. He took off his shoes and replaced them with the pair of old sneakers he'd brought with him. He hadn't worn them in so many years, he couldn't remember the last time. He had considered bringing something to change into as well when he packed the sneakers then realized he didn't have anything. There was nothing in his closet or his drawers but the regulation dark suit and white shirt he wore every day. The sneakers felt surprising good on his feet. "Shall we?" he said.

"Sure," Carlos replied.

"Are there any rules I need to know about?" Shalom asked, glancing over at Baruch.

Carlos smiled. "It's really simple. Everyone gets a turn. That pattern, the ritual, makes it easier for Baruch to follow."

"I see," he said, acknowledging what Carlos told him as if he already knew it." Shalom felt sad. He realized how unaware he was about his son's life and character. In that way, he was too much like his own father.

"Like this," Carlos said, tossing the ball on a bounce to Baruch. "Your turn."

Baruch dribbled the ball a bit then trotted up to the basket for a lay-up. The ball dropped through the net and bounced after hitting the concrete. Baruch retrieved it and passed it back to Carlos. Carlos took the ball and retraced Baruch's steps, rebounding the lay-up off the backboard. Baruch laughed with glee and clapped his hands as the ball swept through the net a second time.

"Okay, Rabbi, your turn," Carlos said as he retrieved the ball and tossed it to Shalom.

As Shalom took the ball and dribbled tentatively, a look of confusion came over Baruch's face, along with a guttural moan. Shalom stopped, his first instinct to run to Baruch and calm him. Instead, he stopped himself. He watched Carlos as he put one hand on Baruch's upper arm, barely touching him. Baruch calmed almost instantly.

"What's wrong?" Carlos asked. Baruch remained silent, glancing off in the opposite direction. "Remember? I explained this to you. Your papa wants to play with us. You'll have your turn next."

A look of understanding crossed Baruch's face, followed a moment later by a smile. He looked at Shalom. The word papa came from his lips.

"Rabbi, now," said Carlos, gesturing with some urgency toward the net.

Shalom dribbled the ball again, this time more aggressively and took a tentative step, then another toward the basket. He hadn't tossed a basketball in nearly thirty years. As he neared the basket, he pushed the ball off his left palm with his right hand. He felt a moment of panic in his chest as the ball launched upward. He held his breath, wanting this to go well. Shalom let out a sigh of relief as the ball bounced off the backboard and through the net. Baruch clapped as the ball hit the pavement. Shalom retrieved it and bounced it to Baruch who took it and made another shot, this time from the foul line.

"He picks his positions," Carlos shouted to Shalom from the other side of the court, as Baruch passed him the ball. Carlos made the same shot and passed the ball to Shalom. This time Baruch didn't flinch. Shalom knew what to do. As his shot sailed through the net, Baruch clapped again.

಄಄಄

Shalom looked over at the construction site as they exited the schoolyard. He could almost see the ghosts moving in and out of the house, his father, Erno, their tenants, and, in particular, that guy whose picture the detectives had shown him. He hadn't liked that man from the first time he saw him.

Bronx, NYC
May 1966

It had been no small task to get his father to a Yankee game. In the end, it was Uncle Erno who made it happen. Erno was always there for Stephen, understanding his needs when his father didn't.

It was clear to Stephen that his father knew absolutely nothing about baseball and had no desire to learn. Mostly, Stephen recognized, his father was never comfortable in situations where he wasn't familiar with the surroundings. Yankee Stadium was one of those situations.

Stephen walked up the inclined ramp toward the seats. Through the end of the passage, like a big, framed window, he could see the other side of the stadium, the blue seats tiny and far away. As he grew closer to the end of the passageway the sunlight intensified and the roar of tens of thousands of people magnified. Then, as Stephen reached the end of the passage, the vista opened. The emerald green field rimmed by rich, leathery-brown earth exploded before him. He had seen it many times on television in their living room in black and white. It never looked like this. It was enormous. Stephen stopped dead in his tracks. He felt his father's hand on his shoulder. "Do you like it?" he said.

Stephen turned to him. His father was smiling broadly. "Like it? You can't imagine how much I wanted to come here."

Erno handed Stephen the tickets. "Go ahead, find our seats," he said, pointing to the players scrambling onto the field. "Looks like the game is going to start soon."

Stephen looked at the row and seat numbers on the tickets and scanned the seats. He wasn't sure how to find them.

"May I help you?" said a man with a Yankees shirt and cap.

"I'm trying to find our seats."

The usher took the tickets. "Right this way." He led them up two rows and pointed to the first three seats.

"Thanks," Stephen said. Erno thanked the usher as well and slipped something into his hand. Stephen thought to ask about it but decided not to.

"Sit between us," his father said.

As they sat down, the announcer asked everyone to stand for the national anthem. Stephen removed his Yankee cap and placed his hand over his heart and sang along. He looked at both his father and Erno. To his surprise they both knew the words. Stephen was proud. He loved them both, especially his father. He always wanted them to be American and rarely felt they were. But today was different. They were as American as him and everyone else.

The crowd applauded as the first ball was pitched. "That's the pitcher in the center," Stephen said, explaining the game to them. Both Max and Erno laughed. "We know," said Max. "They love baseball in the Dominican Republic."

Stephen was surprised. He had never so much as had a catch with his father. "Did you play?"

"We played once," Erno said, he and Max laughing again, this time more deeply, exchanging knowing glances. Stephen wanted to know more but was afraid to ask. He knew how any questions about their past could change the mood from happy to mournful in a tiny moment.

"It was hopeless," Max said, without Stephen's prompting. "One doesn't learn to play baseball as an adult."

The first half of the first inning was over quickly, one, two, three. The Yankees came up to bat. The crack of bat against ball shattered the conversation. Seated in the second tier halfway between home base and third, Stephen watched as a home run sailed out of the park. "That's why they called them the Bronx Bombers." He jumped out of his seat and cheered.

As he sat back down, he felt his father's arm rest across his shoulder. He hesitated for a moment. For once, mention of the past hadn't changed his father's mood. Stephen wanted to ask them more about baseball and the Dominican Republic. He wondered how far he could go with his questions. "Why didn't you learn to play baseball when you were a kid?"

"We didn't play baseball in Hungary," Max said, still light and open.

"What did you play?" Stephen asked, emboldened by his father's upbeat response.

"We didn't play anything."

"Why?"

Max wavered for a moment. He didn't like to talk about his childhood. Every moment of it was filled with the memory of his twin brother. No matter how much time passed, that wound that would never heal.

"Your father was a poor boy," Erno said, rescuing Max. "There was no time for playing anything."

Max smiled. "We went to school and then we helped our parents in their store."

"They had a store?" Steven said. This was the most information he had ever learned about his grandparents, other than that they had died in Europe during "the war." Pictures of his grandparents, and his aunts, uncles, and cousins, hung on the wall in the long, dark foyer that led from the front door of the apartment to the living room. They stood silently like ghostly sentinels watching over their apartment along with his mother's family on the opposing wall.

At the end of the hall nearest to the living room were two photographs that shared one frame. One was of his father with his twin brother Istvan—for whom Stephen was named—when they were boys. They stood in front of an old wood house in short pants their arms over each other's shoulders. They were about Stephen's age in that photo. They smiled broadly without a care in the world. In the other photo they were grown men, sharing a stone bench in a park. His mother told him the second photo was taken in Genoa, Italy. There were two women in the photo with his father and his uncle, his mother and a woman he assumed was his uncle's wife. They wore heavy coats and looked very unhappy. His mother told him it was taken on their way to the Dominican Republic. Whenever he looked at that photograph, Stephen wondered why his uncle never got to the Dominican Republic.

"Yes, we had a store," Max answered, after a long moment.

"What kind of store?"

Max looked to Erno. His eyes pleaded with him to distract Stephen. This time Erno didn't. "Tell him," he said in Hungarian. "He needs to know something of who you were, where he comes from."

Max knew Erno was right. He had to open up to Stephen. A person needed to know where they came from. He thought fondly for a moment of his parents, picturing them standing behind the counter in the store. "It was a general store," Max said. "They sold everything you would need in a small village. And they made liquor."

Stephen's eyes lit up. "How do you make liquor?"

"We made something called *slivovitz*," Max replied. "It's made from plums."

Erno laughed. "And it stinks when you make it!"

There was another crack of the bat and another long shot. This time it was a double and scored two runs. "That's enough talk of the past," Max said, seeking to escape it. "We came to watch the game."

"Okay," said Stephen. He leaned back into his seat. He felt his father's arm settle comfortably onto his shoulder. He smiled.

At the end of the seventh inning, after the crowd sang "Take Me Out to the Ballgame," Max asked Stephen if he wanted another hot dog.

"Yes," Stephen replied.

"Do you think you can get it, or do you want me to go with you?" Max asked.

"I can do it, papa." He liked the idea of going on his own.

Max handed Stephen some money. "Bring me one too. Do you want one Erno?"

"No."

Stephen walked down the long hallway back into the stadium. He stopped at the men's room. While washing his hands at the sink he looked to his left. A man was talking very loudly in Spanish. It wasn't unusual to hear many different languages anywhere in New York City. But he knew this voice. It was the new boarder, the guy his father introduced him to, Fernando Vargas. He tried to pass without being seen. He didn't want to have to talk to him.

"Stephen?" he heard, thinking he had escaped detection.

As he turned to open the door, he smiled. "Hi."

"You father is here?"

Stephen had no choice. He knew no one would believe he was here alone, not even this man. He was too young. "Yes, and my uncle." Vargas approached him, the man with whom Vargas had been speaking with in tow. "We come with you to say hello."

Stephen's stomach turned. "I have to pick up hot dogs."

Vargas laughed. Stephen sensed something menacing and insincere about it. "Where are the seats?" Vargas asked.

Stephen knew where to go, how to get back, but didn't know the section number.

"Okay, we wait and go with you," Vargas said, becoming impatient. He said something to the other man in Spanish.

After picking up the hotdogs, Stephen headed back to the seats, Vargas and his friend close behind him. By the time they arrived Stephens' stomach was in a knot. He watched his father's face turn pale as he stared at Vargas and the other man.

Vargas introduced his friend to Max. The man offered his hand. Max hesitated than accepted it without a word. Erno stood up and shook the hands of Vargas and his friend too. The conversation was in Spanish. Though he understood a good deal of what was said, Stephen tuned it out. This man who Stephen found so distasteful was ruining the day. After what felt like an eternity, they left. His father sat down, as did uncle Erno.

Stephen passed the hotdog to Max, then devoured his. He noticed half an inning later his father still hadn't eaten his. "Aren't you hungry, Pop?"

"Not anymore," Max said.

"Are you okay?"

"I'm fine," Max said, though his mood had changed irrevocably. The arm that had rested on Stephen's shoulder now sat crossed against his chest. Stephen hated Vargas and that rooming house. He hated anything that drew his father away from him.

છગ્ચ

Shalom knocked tentatively on Erno's door. He felt a bit embarrassed. Erno was an old man, very old, someone who had been an important part of his life, and he knew he should make more of an effort to see him. If Erno were a member of the synagogue's community, Shalom knew he would visit regularly, no matter how uncomfortable he felt. He forced a smile as the door opened. "*Hola*, Anisa."

"Rabbi, how are you?" Is señor Enrique expecting you?"

"No, I should have called first. Is he awake?"

"Yes. He is having his dinner. He's in the living room. You remember the way?"

"Of course." As Shalom walked down the hall he stopped and glanced quickly at one particular photo on the wall. There was his father, smiling in a way he rarely remembered seeing him, the palm trees waving at his back, dressed in white shirt and pants with Erno and that Dominican friend of his. Shalom felt sad. Why hadn't his father ever been happy in his own memories, here in New York?

"What a surprise," Erno said, Shalom entering the living room.

"I'm sorry it's been so long since I've seen you."

Erno gestured to the couch. "Nonsense, please, sit down."

Shalom sat in the corner of the couch opposite Erno in his wheelchair. "My apologies again."

"Stop, if you apologize again, I will ask you to leave. Can I get you something to drink?"

Shalom hesitated.

"The water is kosher, Stephen."

The joke made Shalom laugh, despite the use of his English name, which he disliked. "Okay."

"Anisa," Erno called out. "*Un vaso de agua, para el rabbi.*"

"*Sí, pronto,*" she called back from the kitchen.

"You know why I'm here?" Shalom asked in Hungarian.

"Of course, I do." Erno replied in English. He put down his fork on the tray that rested on the arms of the wheelchair. "They've been here twice."

"I just don't understand. After almost 40 years, why are they even bothering?"

"It's their job."

"He was an evil man."

"Very much so, but that's not what they care about. Anyway, no one remembers that anymore. It's a footnote in history. You say Trujillo and people look at you like you're speaking Chinese."

"He destroyed my father."

"I know, I was there. I've told them everything they need to know. I told them I did it, I murdered that excuse for human scum. What will they do now? Arrest a ninety-nine-year-old man for a forty-year-old murder?"

Shalom took in a deep breath, his chest rising and falling slowly with it. Sweating despite the air conditioning, Shalom pulled his handkerchief from his pocket and wiped his brow. "Okay," he said. "Perhaps I need to get on with my life then. Thank you Erno-*bacsi.*"

"You're welcome, *mijo.* And that would be a good idea Stephen, getting on with your life. But know this for certain. Your father loved you."

Chapter 18
Washington Heights, NYC
11 August 2008
9:30 a.m.

S o," said Pete, "what we know is that Tejada slipped out of the Dominican Republic and landed here as Vargas and at least part of the time might have claimed to be Cuban."

"True. Which leads to other questions."

Pete took a pad from inside the desk drawer. "Shoot."

"Okay. One, was it easier to enter the U.S. as a Cuban than as a Dominican in sixty-five or sixty-six?"

"I'm pretty sure the Cubans had the right to claim political asylum immediately upon entering the country by then."

"We need to check the effective date on that."

"Got it." Pete made a note on the pad. "The other possibility is that he had help coming in from Santo Domingo."

"What you mean?" Tolya said.

Pete loved to fill in the facts he'd accumulated for Tolya. "The American government was afraid of a communist takeover when the civil war erupted in the DR in sixty-four. Perhaps the CIA helped some of these guys to get out when the anti-Trujillo forces were in control."

"If that's the case, why would they have given him a Cuban identity?"

"To give him a new life altogether."

"Good point."

"How do we check into that?"

"We could try immigration records. I'll get on that."

"There's one other thing."

"What?"

Tolya pulled out one of the diaries from his bag. "Look at this." He pointed to the date in Roman numerals at the top of one of the entries. Then at another.

"Explain."

They're not chronological dates. They jump around, and they correspond to some of the date entries in the other diaries, and they're in Hungarian."

Pete examined the entry Tolya had pointed out as well as the ones immediately following and proceeding. "He makes separate entries for the same dates in different languages and in different diaries?"

"Appears that way."

"Is it a security system?"

"I think so. I think our answer is in this volume."

"We can't use Erno again. Where are we gonna find someone to translate this?" Pete asked.

"Actually, I was thinking we should call your friend at CUNY and get a referral to someone who teaches Hungarian."

"Good point." Pete picked up the handset from his desk phone and dialed Tejada's number.

⟡⟡⟡

Tolya stood outside the door of Assistant Professor Evangeline Anderson's office. He turned the doorknob and pushed in slowly. An attractive black woman of in her mid-40's sat behind a desk. She looked up at him and smiled. "Can I help you?"

"Professor Anderson?"

"Yes,"

Tolya smiled. He closed the door behind him. "I'm Detective Kurchenko. My partner, Pete Gonzalvez, spoke with you about an hour ago."

"Yes. Please, sit down." The Professor smiled broadly as she got up from her chair and offered Tolya her hand. She was tall and thin, perhaps 5'10", dressed in jeans and a pink T-shirt. "Don't be embarrassed, Detective," she said. "I know what you're thinking. It happens all the time. How can a professor of Eastern European languages be a black woman?"

Tolya felt himself blush. "I'm sorry, I didn't mean…"

"No, no, I get that all the time. Russky?" she asked.

"Yes," replied Tolya. He was caught off guard. "You speak Russian as well?" he asked in Russian.

"*Da.*" She pointed to the door and laughed. "It says Eastern European languages."

"*Pravda.*" Tolya let himself relax as he sat down opposite her. "Can I ask how you came to this line of work?" he said, continuing in Russian…

"Sure. It's really quite simple. I was a young, black, woman studying foreign affairs and I wanted to stand out from the crowd. Condoleeza Rice was my role model, and I thought, why not? I learned Russian, Hungarian, and Polish. Then Communism collapsed. I tried Academia, liked it and stayed."

"Fascinating."

"May I see what you've got?" Professor Anderson said switching back to English. She pointed to the diary in Tolya's hand. "I don't want to rush you, but I've got a faculty meeting in half an hour."

Tolya handed her the thin, gray-leather volume. "This is a diary written by a suspect in a cold case from nineteen-sixty-six. We think it might contain some leads."

The professor took the diary from Tolya. She thumbed through it and shook her head. "I'm sorry Detective. This isn't Hungarian. It looks like Slovak."

"Wow, I don't suppose you speak Slovak too?"

"No, but my colleague down the hall does. His name is Anton Dvorak. He's four doors down. Go there and knock. Tell him I sent you."

Tolya waited at the Caridad, sipping his Dominican coffee. Pete was, as usual, late. After their recent Mexican lunch debacle, Pete was insisting on Dominican only. It went well with the investigation anyway, sort of fit into the spirit of the suspects and the victim. Tolya glanced at the blackboard above the steam table for today's lunch specials, *pescado con coco*. Perfect, his favorite.

Pete swaggered in waving a handful of papers. Tolya signaled to him from the back corner.

"Brotherman," Pete said, a little out of breath.

"What's up?"

"I got us some answers. You're not going to believe this shit."

The waitress interrupted them. Pete looked up at her. "*Quiero un Cubano, y un orden de tostones. Y dos Presidentes.*"

"I don't want a beer," said Tolya.

"Who said the second one is for you?" Pete laughed. "You're gonna want one, take my word."

"Okay."

"*Y tú?*" asked the waitress pivoting to Tolya.

"*El especiál, pescado con coco.*"

Pete laughed again as the waitress ran off. "We turned you into a real Dominican, me and your wife."

Tolya laughed as well. "*Sí.* Now tell me what you learned."

The waitress returned with the beers. They tapped the necks of their bottles twice, once on each side, as they always did. Pete took a long swig.

"Well, you gonna tell me?" Tolya said, staring at Pete downing his beer.

"Sure," Pete said, letting out a huge belch. "I tried to get some info on the net and there wasn't much there. Bullshit, you know, the kind for civies."

"Civies?"

"Yeah, civilians."

"Did you go onto the department intranet? Cooperating agencies?"

"Yeah, of course. It was, leave a message, we'll get back to you. We need this info now. So, I called my nephew, the one that just got out of the service."

"And?"

"His buddy is still in, re-enlisted. He's in military intelligence, in Virginia. He hooked me up."

"Just like that?"

"Yeah, *Dominicano a Dominicano.* You know how we are." Pete smiled broadly, leaned back and took another long swig on his beer.

Tolya shook his head. "I sure do. What did he tell you?"

"He hooked me up with this guy who's a military historian with their intel department. He said off the record that the U.S. Military did the same for Trujillo's murderers that it did for scumbags all over the world and still does. If you helped out, or if you had the right friends, they got you out."

"He's sure about this? This shit isn't some kind of classified?"

"It's low-level shit now. Nobody cares about Trujillo anymore. I gave him the info and said he'd call me back in like an hour and a half. He was like clockwork. That's why I was late."

"Bullshit, that's not why you were late. You're always late." Pete laughed. Tolya loved to see him like this, how juiced up he got when he dove deep into a case.

The waitress arrived with their lunches and placed them on the table. "*Algo mas?*"

"*Sí, una cerveza mas, bien fría, por favor,*" Pete said as he chugged down the remainder of his bottle. "*Dos.*" He gestured to Tolya's bottle which was still half full. "*Gracias*."

"Anyway, he called me from his cell, from outside his office, so he could talk freely. Here's the deal." Pete leaned over the table, his elbows on either side of his plate, his eyes on fire. "Our government was crazy nervous that Bosch would take Santo Domingo communist the way Castro had done in Cuba, so they landed marines in sixty-five to squash the revolt in favor of Balenguer, who was Trujillo's man. Meantime, they had Tejada on the payroll from years before. He worked for Trujillo, but he also worked for the Americans, keeping an eye on who was doing what for who, and for how much. You might say they were protecting their investment. So, when they came in sixty-five, and they helped dump Bosch, they also knew there were a few guys who were compromised, including our boy. If the anti-Trujillistas didn't get him, the Trujillistas would kill him when they found out he was working for the Americans. Everything was out."

"So, they gave him a new identity and sent him here?"

"*Exacto*. And they made him Cuban for extra cover. But he wasn't so good at keeping that cover."

"Miriam Rivera."

"*Sí*, and our boys were right, it was him."

"Looks that way." Pete lifted his beer to Tolya. They clicked their bottles twice again. Pete picked up half of the sandwich. "What did you find out?" Pete asked as he bit off a huge chunk of the sandwich.

"The diary isn't in Hungarian."

Pete's eyes widened. "What?" he said through a mouth full of Cubano.

"It's in Slovak."

"How many languages this guy spoke?"

"More than us."

"What did you do?"

"The Hungarian professor sent me down the hall to her colleague, who is reading it as we speak."

"When will he have it?"

"He said he would get back to me by Wednesday with as much as he can."

"What are we doing in the meantime?"

Tolya pushed the remainder of his fish into the pile of black beans and white rice. "I think we'll make another visit to Erno this afternoon after we finish lunch and then, my brother, I'm taking my wife and son to the beach tomorrow. I've worked the last two weekends and tomorrow is supposed to be the most perfect day of the summer. Karin is insisting that this forty-year-old murder can wait one more day to be solved."

◐◑◐

The voicemail light was flashing on Pete's desk phone when they got back from lunch. He listened to the message. "What time is it, Tol?" he asked as he finished scribbling down the number.

"Two-thirty."

"Damn."

"What?"

"It's the handwriting guy. He said he's there till two." Pete dialed the number. On the third ring, someone picked up.

"Is Mr. Wayne in?"

"No, sorry, he left about a half hour ago."

"Who's this?"

"His service."

"Does he have a cell?"

"I'm not allowed to give that out."

"This is Detective Pete Gonzalvez of the NYPD."

There was silence for a moment. "How do I know that you're telling me the truth?"

Pete became irritated. He put his hand over the mouthpiece. "I'm tired of dealing with idiots." He handed the phone to Tolya.

"This is Detective Kurchenko," Tolya said. "We're returning Mr. Wayne's call. It's very important. Can you get him on the phone?" There was another silence.

"I can try to reach him. Hold please."

"Well?" Pete said.

"Now I'm on hold."

"Who has an answering service anymore?" Pete said.

A moment later the woman came back on. "Hold for Mr. Wayne please." Tolya handed the phone back to Pete.

"This is Marshal Wayne."

"Detective Gonzalvez here."

"Detective, I'm sorry, I waited for you till two-twenty."

"We were at lunch. Do you have the results?"

"Yes. I'm pretty certain, ninety-nine percent, that the two samples are the same. Very interesting stuff, unusual.

They were written by someone who was educated in central Europe in the first few decades of the twentieth century, before the war. You can tell from the very unusual form of cursive he uses. Do you know the identity of the writer?"

"We sure do." Pete nodded at Tolya. They're the same, he mouthed. "Thanks. Send us your report ASAP please. We'll call if we have any more questions."

"It's early," Tolya said, checking his watch. "let's go see Erno. I told you, I wanna finish this up today. I'm going to the beach tomorrow."

Chapter 19

Washington Heights, NYC
11 August 2008
3:30 p.m.

Though Erno looked directly at Tolya and Pete, his eyes were clearly seeing events as they had happened a half-century earlier. It was as if he was watching those events unfold right in front of his eyes again. He neither smiled nor showed any sense of sadness. He was nothing more than an observer. "Yes, as I told you," he said, after a long silence, "I killed him. Believe me, he deserved it. You are correct. Max wrote the note. We had to think fast. We were scared to death."

Tolya considered Erno's statement before responding. He found it hard to believe that either Max or Erno would be afraid of anything. They had escaped the Nazis, survived in a jungle, and outsmarted Trujillo's henchmen. "Why didn't you just go to the police and report what happened? It was, for all intents, self-defense."

Erno closed his eyes and settled deeper into the wheelchair. He pulled the soft cotton blanket that covered him closer. "We were afraid of the police. Remember where we came from, not places where the police were there to help, or protect us."

"We understand that," Pete said. He leaned forward, his elbows on his knees, his hands clasped. "Just so we understand the sequence of events, let me run through this again." Pete picked up his pen and pad, and tapped on his notes, paraphrasing as he went. "You and Max confronted Vargas, or Tejada, or whatever his name was. He pulled a gun. You charged him and grabbed the gun. In the scuffle, the gun went off and he was wounded. He died shortly thereafter. You buried him in the wall. The following day his girlfriend came around looking for him. Max told her neither of you had seen him. Then Max realized she'd keep coming back, so you gave her the note, which Max wrote."

"Yes."

"And the note was in English because…"

Erno nodded his head almost imperceptibly. "All correct. We discussed that at the time. We were going to write it in Spanish, but then we decided that the note was really for the police, not the girlfriend. We knew they would see it, and there weren't any police in the neighborhood who could speak or read Spanish. The police didn't know him. They didn't know that he could barely speak English. There was no way they would figure that out. And our English was bad enough that the note looked like it came from someone who didn't speak or write English well." Erno lifted his head and looked from Tolya to Pete and back again. "It made sense, at the time."

Tolya was concerned by the amount of thought that had gone into this. It reeked of pre-meditation. "One more question, Erno. Why did you write in the note that he was going to Florida and taking his girlfriend with him? You knew she was around the corner."

Erno let out a long sigh. "We thought a lot about that too."

Washington Heights, NYC
July 4, 1966

Erno dumped Vargas' body on the floor in his room. He leaned against the wall, out of breath from carrying it up two flights. Vargas' blood seeped along the floorboards, discoloring the wood. It had dripped everywhere on the way up from the first floor as well. Erno felt no sadness for the motionless mass at his feet. He wanted only to make it go away, regretting the moment he saw Tejada on St. Nicholas Avenue to begin with. He was sorry he followed him to the bank. He was sorry he'd ever told Max. What good could have come of this? None. He knew that now. They were in deep trouble. Deeper trouble than either of them were equipped to handle. Erno clenched his fists, his anger overwhelming. He kicked the body, the blood splattering on his clothes. "You are a cancer, you and your kind, fascist." Erno spat at the body, the wad of saliva landing on Tejada's face.

"Erno," Max shouted as he came up the stairs. He handed him a sledgehammer and laid down a bag of tools near the corner of the two walls. "Okay let's get to work. I paid the kids in the street to set off fireworks. They've got about twenty minutes worth. We have to take down that wall before they finish. The noise will cover up the banging."

"What are you talking about?"

"We're going to bury him in the wall."

Erno stopped dead in his tracks, his right hand against the wall for support. "What?" he said. His mind was swirling around like hurricane force winds. "Max, no, that's crazy." He put his other hand on Max's shoulder. "We have to call the police."

"The police? No, definitely not." Max picked up the sledgehammer and swung it over his shoulder. "Someone will have to go to prison for this. He's ruined my life once. I'm not going to let him ruin it again."

Erno slipped into the corner next to the armoire. He felt as if he were going to pass out. "I can't do this."

Max let the sledgehammer slip to the floor with a thud. He placed his palm on top of the handle and leaned on it, staring at Erno. Erno was frightened by the look in Max's eyes, dead, emotionless, like the day he found him in the wreckage at José's house. Max was calm, too calm, and too impatient to finish the job. "Then why did you tell me about him to begin with? Did you think I would do nothing?"

Erno felt like he was about to vomit. He looked again at Tejada's' blood seeping into the wood floorboards and swallowed hard to keep his stomach from cramping. "I don't know. I shouldn't have. Look what's happened."

"Did you think I had forgotten? I relive that day every night of my life." Max picked up the sledgehammer again, swinging it toward the wall to judge its weight and his balance. "We have to finish this."

"I can't." Erno looked at Tejada's face again, gaunt and frightened, his mouth agape. "I think he's still breathing."

Max placed his finger against Vargas' neck. "There's no pulse. And even if there was, he wouldn't last long. And why should I care? Did he care about Anabela? Or José? Or Nereida?" He hesitated for a moment. "Or me!" he screamed.

Erno hesitated. Max's eyes were ablaze with hate and satisfaction. Erno knew there was nothing he could do to dissuade him. "I understand," he said, almost a whisper. "But I can't do this."

"Then watch me." Max turned his back to Erno and sized up the wall.

"You were always the strong one," said Erno.

"Yes, I was," Max replied. "And I forgive you brother, I understand. The truth is this was always my fight and mine alone. I have to finish this now."

A moment later the sound of firecrackers shattered the silence between them. Max swung the sledgehammer, slamming it into the plaster wall. The paint and plaster and chips of wood crumbled and scattered easily, dust everywhere. Max kept slamming the wall till he had an opening the size of a man. There was enough space inside between the lathe and the outer bricks to fit a body snugly. Max stepped back from his handy work. "Erno, go down to the kitchen and bring one of the wood chairs, please."

Erno hesitated.

Max turned to him. "Please, I have a lot to do."

Erno ran down the stairs to the first floor and grabbed one of the extra chairs they left against the wall for when they needed more seating at the dining table. He would come up with a story for Ava later when she asked what had become of it. It rarely got used anyway. He took a deep breath then shuddered. He had no choice but to help Max.

This was his fault. He had brought Tejada to them. Max was right. Best to finish this quickly.

Erno took the steps two at a time back to the third floor, breathless by the time he reached the top. Max had cleared the debris from in front of the wall in those few moments. Erno couldn't imagine where Max found the strength. "Here," he said, handing the chair to him.

Max wedged it into the space between the outer and inner walls. "All right," he pointed, "we need to put him in here."

"And then?"

"I'm going to repair the wall."

"What about the blood here, and in the dining room, and everywhere else?"

"We'll clean it up."

"When? And what are we going to tell our wives? This will take all night."

Max thought for a moment. He took a deep breath and closed his eyes. "You're right. Let's get this part done. We have to get rid of the body now. We can take care of the rest tomorrow. No one will be coming into the house. We have no tenants, remember?"

"This will take hours."

Max smiled, his expression calm, almost tranquil. "It certainly will if we keep discussing it. Help me with the body."

Erno operated reactively. He did as Max asked, putting his hands under Vargas' shoulders, the sticky wetness of his blood congealing in Erno's palms, warm and sickening. Max took Vargas' legs. "All right, let's sit him in the chair."

Erno felt his knees begin to shake. He willed himself to calm down. He owed Max this much. "One, two, three," Max said. They lifted the body and carried it the few feet to the hole in the wall, placing it on the chair.

Max pointed to the dresser. "Give me that."

Erno reached for Vargas' hat and handed it to Max. Max placed it on the dead man's head. "He'll be properly dressed when he gets to hell," Max said, laughing. Erno nearly fainted.

Erno returned to the rooming house at 3 a.m. He found Max in the dining room cleaning the floor of blood. "How do you know how to do this?" he asked.

Max laughed. "If you had worked in the slaughterhouse in the settlement you'd know how too. But a bon vivant like you…"

Erno thought to laugh as well. What Max had said was funny, but then he stopped himself. Laughter didn't fit into this picture.

"What did you tell Helen and Ava?"

"I told them we discovered a leak in the sewage pipe in the basement. That we called the plumber and he was coming and that you needed to wait for him. That he told us he would need one of us to help him, so you insisted I go to the party and that you would stay."

"Did Helen believe you?"

"I suppose so."

Max doubted it. Helen always suspected something when he was absent. But then he couldn't blame her, though he hadn't had a girlfriend since they'd left Santo

Domingo. She was always suspicious. He'd made a promise to himself and he'd kept it, no more women.

"And Stephen?"

"Asleep in his room. I checked before I went to the party to find Helen and Ava."

"I'm done here for now. I'm going home," Max said. Erno saw both stress and relief in Max's face. Max looked directly into Erno's eyes, his face as hard as stone. "This is done, finally," Max said. "We'll never speak of this again."

The following day Max was in the dining room repairing the wall where the bullet had torn through the wood wainscoting. Erno had given Ava the day off. With only one tenant, one who was now a permanent resident in the back wall of the back room on the third floor, she didn't need to prepare lunch. Tomorrow they would tell her that he had run off. Then they would tell both Ava and Helen that they were putting the building up for sale, no more rooming house. They would be delighted. He would cover all their tracks.

When he heard the door rattle, Max was surprised. He wasn't expecting anyone and Erno had a key. "Who's there?" he called out in English.

The answer came back in Spanish. It was Vargas' girlfriend. He disliked the Puerto Rican woman simply for the fact that she was Vargas' girlfriend, and besides she was very nosey. Max went to the door.

"*Hola.*"

"Máximo, why is the door locked?"

"I don't know," he lied. He checked the inside tumbler on the lock to make his response seem genuine. "Someone must have locked it without me knowing."

"Have you seen Nando?" Miriam asked.

"No, I thought he was with you," Max lied.

Miriam turned away. She put her hand to her mouth as she spoke. "We were supposed to go to the park last night for the fireworks. He never came for me." Max heard the emotion in her voice. Tears were forming in her eyes. He felt his stomach tighten with a sense of pity for this woman. He knew her feeling of desperate alarm. But why should he care, considering what Tejada had taken from him. "He's not here."

"Can I go to his room?"

"It's locked. That's why I thought he was with you."

She backed off and began to walk away, a tissue in her right hand, which she dabbed at her nose and eyes. "Please, tell him I was here."

∾◦∾

"She'll be back," Erno said.

"I know," Max replied.

"What are we going to do?"

"I've been thinking about that. We have to make it look like he left. Get rid of his things. If she goes to the police and they come looking for him, we'll tell them he ran out in the middle of the night. We'll say he left a note."

"And what if they want to see the note?"

"We'll show it to them."

"We don't have one."

"We'll write one."

Max went to the desk in the living room and reached into the middle draw, filled with paper and pens and envelopes for the boarders. He took out a sheet.

"What are you going to write?"

"I'm not sure, but we'll come up with something." Max hesitated for a moment. "What language should this be in?" he said.

"He only speaks Spanish."

"But the cops only speak English."

"But he didn't."

"But they don't know that."

Erno hesitated. "English then."

Max sat down at the desk and began to write. He stopped after several lines, read the letter and then tore it up. He would burn the scraps latter. He started again, Erno watching him nervously. After several minutes he stopped and read the letter out loud. "Much better," he said and handed the letter to Erno.

Erno read over the letter. "Max, why did you put that he was going to take the girlfriend with him? She's here."

"To make her angry with him. He left her. She'll stop coming around." But Max knew he was wrong even then. He knew one thing for certain. No one ever stops searching for lost love.

Chapter 20
Long Beach, NYC
12 August 2008
11:30 a.m.

Tolya settled into his sand chair. He laid back and let out his breath slowly, pushing the chair down, stretching his legs. The warm sand soothed his heels It was the perfect beach day. Despite his fair complexion he loved the warmth of the sun against his skin. He always did.

A memory passed through his mind so vividly he could almost reach out and touch it. He was eight years old. He and Oleg were running down the beach in Crimea, on the shores of the Black Sea. His father was calling after them to come back. It was time for lunch. They had the use of an elegant *dacha* on the water. His father was rewarded for the work he had done for the glory of the Soviet Union with a vacation. That was before his father fell out of favor and was expelled from the Party. Their next vacation would be in Siberia.

"Is he asleep?" asked Karin, pulling Tolya back to the here and now. She was stretched out on a lounger. Karin made no effort to conceal her pregnancy. Her bathing suit, though made for a woman in her last months, revealed not only that she was pregnant, but also her long, shapely legs, and her now swollen breasts. Tolya loved her this way. Her sexiness was multiplied for him by the fact that she was carrying his child.

Tolya peered into the baby tent just behind them. Max lay quietly, his pacifier half out of his mouth. A gentle breeze flapped the pink and yellow parachute material that hung from the tent and functioned as a door of sorts. It could be zipped shut if the wind picked up. "Yes," he replied. "He could sleep through a nuclear attack." Tolya reached over and took her hand. "I love you."

Karin smiled. "I know that."

Tolya feigned insult. He let go of her hand and made a face. "You could say you love me, too."

"You already know that." She took his hand back and kissed it gently, before placing it on her stomach. "Have you decided on a name yet?"

Tolya tensed slightly. "Do we have to talk about that today?" The breeze carried a bit of the spray from the surf to his face. "I'm here to relax."

"This case has you crazy. Exactly like you were with Máximo. Could you hand me the container with the grapes please?"

Tolya reached behind him and grabbed the container Karin had packed full of fresh grapes—green, red, and black—and handed it to her in one swift movement. "It's those diaries. It's all that conflict Max has with his past." He hesitated. "It's his issues with his dead twin, and you want to know why it makes me tense?"

"I understand, *amor*," said Karin. She took his hand in hers again. "Like last time, too close for comfort. But you're not him. You never even knew him. He's like a character in a book."

"It's just too close, too familiar. And you want to know if I've thought about a name?"

"Yes, I do. I'd like to know what our son will be named." She broke off a branch of black grapes and put one in her mouth, slowly pressing the juice out onto her tongue. "Here, try these, *que rico*." She popped one in Tolya's mouth.

The juice exploded on his tongue as he bit down on the grape. "Sweet," he said swallowing the pulp.

"So, I ask you again. Have you considered a name?"

Though the beach had immediately calmed him, Tolya felt the tension return with this conversation. "I have."

"Do you want to share it with me?"

"I'm not sure,"

"Not sure of what? Whether you want to share it with me or what name you prefer?"

Tolya chuckled. "You're too tough on me, woman."

Karin squeezed his hand. "To repeat, I'd like to know what my son's name will be. And besides, I have to start embroidering it on his baby clothes."

Tolya laughed. "Embroidering? You?" He took some more grapes and popped them in his mouth, this time a mixture of green, red, and black. "I was going to name him Oleg." The combination of the three was both sweet and tart, as was his feeling about his decision.

"I'm fine with that."

"But…" said Tolya.

"But what?"

"Those diaries have me rethinking it."

Karin pulled herself up in the lounge chair. She became deadly serious. "I don't know why you don't just close this case. What is driving you? This murder happened over forty years ago. Erno has confessed." Her voice began to rise. She caught herself and lowered her tone to a whisper, her exasperation still evident. She understood Tolya's need to find the truth. That was what detective work was all about. But she couldn't watch him torture himself with the details. "You know what happened? You have a confession. Just close the case and move on, before it drives you, and me, crazy."

"I can't do that Karin. We've gone too far with this. Both Pete and I are convinced he's lying."

"Why would he lie?"

"He's covering for someone."

Karin shook her head. "My darling, what difference does it make at this point? Whoever it is he's covering for would be long dead by now."

Tolya hesitated a moment. "Perhaps not. Perhaps that's the whole point."

❧❧❧

Shalom poured himself a second cup of coffee from the porcelain set on the low table in Erno's living room. He added a teaspoon of sugar but no cream. He'd had meat for lunch two hours earlier. The smell of Erno's living room, the keepsakes and photographs, reminded him of his parents' apartment, the apartment he'd grown up in. He recalled thinking as a boy what the apartments of other people who had living relatives might have looked like? He'd always thought of his apartment as more like a tomb or a memorial, with too many photos of the dead everywhere. Erno's place was the same. How many memorials like this still existed today, more than sixty years after the war ended?

"I'm happy to hear about Baruch's improvement," said Erno. "How does he cope with his mother's absence?"

Shalom wasn't sure how to respond. The truth was that Baruch's psyche, his inner feelings, were impenetrable. He couldn't tell you himself. Shalom was never certain what was lurking under the surface until it exploded. Most of the time the sea of Baruch's mind appeared tranquil, but occasionally it could turn into a tidal wave, wiping out everything in its path. "He seems to have accepted it," Shalom said. He considered for a moment whether he himself believed that. "But then who knows?"

Erno took a sip of his coffee, the cup shaking a bit from a slight tremor in the old man's hands. "You did the right thing bringing back the young Dominican boy to work with him. He has a way with Baruch, I remember when your father was alive. I would see them together at the park and how well Carlos handled him. I know that wasn't easy for you."

"No," replied Shalom. "And I didn't act with kindness toward him then either. I will always regret that. This is my *kaperet*."

Erno laughed, the soft pangs causing his body to tremble slightly. "I haven't heard that word in probably ninety years."

Perhaps if you hadn't abandoned your faith you might have heard it again, Shalom thought. He kept his opinion to himself.

"Let me tell you a story," Erno said, his face changing with his words, becaming in some way younger as he began to remember. "My father would take me to see his father, my grandfather, in the village where he was born in the weeks before the Jewish New Year, this time of year, every year. It was near the bend of the Danube, a very Hungarian place. My father was completely assimilated, a real Hungarian, but my grandfather was not. Despite the changes for the Jews in Hungary at that time, he remained very observant. He always covered his head. Observed the Sabbath. When my father wasn't paying attention, my grandfather would take me off with him to the cemetery outside the village where his parents were buried. He would make *kaporos* over me to expiate my sins. He would wave a chicken around over my head then slit its neck. When we returned with the carcass, my beloved father, the dedicated son that he was despite all his modernity, behaved as if he thought we had gone to the butcher, but I'm sure he knew what my grandfather was up to. A world vanished."

Shalom smiled but remained silent. He didn't find the story funny at all. He knew many people in his community who still observed this custom.

"Now, my best friend's son, tell me why you are here."

"I just came to visit."

"Excuse me, Rabbi, but that's a load of crap," Erno replied. "You rarely come to visit. I'm delighted to see you, to be sure, but the truth is I haven't seen you this much in more than a decade."

Shalom squirmed in his chair. He did have a reason for his visit. It bounced around in his mind, fighting with him to come out into full view. He just didn't know whether he wanted to open the door.

"Don't misunderstand me," said Erno. "I'm enjoying your company. I always did. You were the closest thing I had to a son. I miss you."

Shalom felt himself blush. He recalled how much he'd loved Erno as a boy. How Erno was a counterpoint to his father. How Erno somehow knew how to be gentle and caring when his father couldn't. Shalom put his cup and saucer down. He leaned forward. He knew Anisa was in the kitchen and probably listening. What he had to ask and the answers that Erno would give him, weren't for her ears. "Who was Vargas?"

A look of sadness came over Erno's face. "It seems this tragedy will never leave us." He too looked toward the kitchen. "How is your Hungarian?" he asked.

"A bit rusty," Shalom said.

Erno smiled. "I remember when you were a boy and your father would speak to you in the street in Hungarian, how angry you would get, but you understood every word."

"How did you know?"

"By your responses in English. They were perfect in either language. What do you want to know?"

"*Mindent*," Shalom replied in Hungarian. "Everything."

"How much did they tell you, your father and mother?"

"My father nothing. He refused to discuss the past. Any time he caught my mother filling in the holes he would stop her. What she did tell me was clearly sanitized."

"Do you know that your parents separated in Santo Domingo?" Erno said, continuing in Hungarian.

"No, I didn't." Shalom felt very uncomfortable, like he was betraying a trust. To discuss this was something like gossip, the *lashon ha-rah*, forbidden by the Torah. He knew his parents' marriage had been less than perfect, but he was unaware that it had nearly ended.

"Do you remember your father mentioning a friend named José?"

"Yes, occasionally. He would get very sad at the mention of that name. Often he would change the subject immediately."

"José was his best friend. He became like a brother to him, particularly after your father learned of his twin brother's death. After your parents separated, your father went to live with him in the village around the bay from Sosúa."

Shalom was shocked. Neither his father nor his mother had ever told him this. It wasn't something he would have ever considered. "He left my mother alone in the jungle?"

"She wasn't exactly alone. There were eight-hundred and fifty other refugees there. And no, that's not what I said, and that's not what happened. Listen to what I'm telling you. They separated. It wasn't his decision alone."

Shalom reached for his coffee and finished what was left in the cup, the coffee already cold.

"Did you know your parents lost a child during a pregnancy in Sosúa?"

"Yes, my mother told me she miscarried due to the primitive conditions."

"That's not exactly how it happened, but it's close enough. They were living on a homestead in the *monte* at that time," Erno continued, using the Dominican term for the jungle-like forest. "We, Ava and I, begged them to come back to the settlement till the baby was born, but your father refused. The baby came early and died in childbirth."

Shalom felt the old feelings of anger toward his father return. His father was often short sighted and impetuous when angry. "That's just like him," Shalom said. "He never considered my mother, her feelings, her safety."

"That's not true," replied Erno. He reached out to Shalom and touched his hand, the translucent skin of his fingers a contrast against Shalom's healthy, pink flesh. "You can't imagine the sadness. You can't imagine the loss. We had escaped from a living hell. We were hounded, pursued, for nothing. Because we were Jews." His voice became stronger, his speech more animated. "That's important to you, Jewishness. It wasn't important to us. It got in our way. We wanted to live, to experience the world. Do you offer more understanding to your congregants because they live a traditional Jewish life than to those of us who choose otherwise?"

Erno's statement stung. Shalom knew Erno was right. He applied a double standard, one for those who observed and another for those who didn't. Shalom felt the coffee churn in his stomach. "I'm sorry Erno-*bacsi*," he said, using the Hungarian diminutive form that roughly meant uncle, "forgive me. It's just that I get very angry with the way my father treated my mother."

"Perhaps you would think of him differently if you knew everything. Shall I continue?"

"Please."

"After the baby died, which happened at exactly the same time as your father learned of the death of his family in Europe, he contracted malaria. He was delirious for weeks. We thought he would die. Ava and I cared for him after he was released from the infirmary. Your mother blamed him for the baby's death. She refused to see him. He blamed himself. She told him to move into the barracks, out of their bungalow. He was unable to work, physically or mentally. He was lost. We worried that he would kill himself. He spent more and more time with José. It was an escape. Eventually he went to live in the village. You have to understand Shalom, more than any of us, more than any other refugee in Sosúa, your father became Dominican. That's how he survived. He shed his broken self and became someone else. Your parents separated. Frankly, your mother told him their marriage was over. He wanted to start over. He couldn't do that in the Sosúa surrounded by every memory, people gossiping. Is that so hard to understand? He had lost everything and everyone. It was a new life or suicide. That wasn't so uncommon in Sosúa."

Erno's words reverberated in Shalom's mind. He still couldn't separate the disappointments of his childhood from the empathy he wanted to feel for his father, the empathy he would show to anyone else. "What happened to him at José's village? Why did he come back?" Shalom asked, the acidity from the coffee crawling ever higher into his throat.

Erno sighed. "They were attacked by Trujillo's henchmen. They killed José and his wife and left your father for dead. I found him in the wreckage of the village, barely breathing and unconscious."

"Why were they attacked?"

Erno drew a breath. He considered how much more should he tell Shalom, how much more did he need to know? He was torn. Was it his to reveal Max's tragedies to Shalom? Shouldn't that have been Max's choice? Hadn't Max made that choice?

"Please, uncle," Shalom said. "I need to understand."

"Trujillo wanted one of the young women from the village for himself. He ordered his men to bring her to him, so he could rape her. Your father and José tried to stop them."

Shalom's mind was in chaos. His father defended the honor of a young woman and nearly died for it. "And who was Vargas?" Shalom asked.

"The man who led the raid. He killed José and his wife Nereida, and others at the village. Except Vargas wasn't his name then. His name was Tejada. He was living here under an assumed name to hide his crimes. We found him, and we made him pay."

Shalom felt like he had been punched in the gut. So much made sense now. But why had his father never been honest with him? What he'd done was heroic. And for that matter, his mother too. "Excuse me for a moment, please."

Shalom walked quickly to the bathroom. He lifted the seat from the toilet and vomited whatever was in his stomach into the bowl as quietly as he could. He stared at himself in the mirror for a moment afterward. He couldn't imagine what their lives had been like in that jungle, a jungle he knew only in his mind. As much as his father claimed to love Santo Domingo, as he referred to it, he never returned and as far as Shalom knew, never so much as thought of taking him to see it. How much had he loved it then, really? Shalom rinsed his mouth and returned to the living room, sweat still beading on his brow.

"Are you all right?" Erno asked.

"Yes, considering," Shalom replied. "Continue, please."

"How much do you remember from that night?"

"What night?"

"The night it happened." Erno cast a quick glance toward the kitchen.

"Not much."

"Tell me what you remember."

Shalom straightened up. He thought for a moment. He had struggled to remove this memory from his mind for more than forty years. A cold shutter slid down his spine, the beads of sweat on his brow collecting and running down into his beard. He took out his handkerchief and wiped his face. "I remember I walked in, there was shouting. You stood between my father and Vargas…"

"Lower your voice and refer to him as *az ember*," that man, in Hungarian.

"Okay."

"Then what do you remember?"

"There was a gun and then a shot. Maybe two. Then there was a lot of blood. After that I remember you grabbing me and taking me out. Then nothing until later that night when you came to check on me."

"What is it you want to know then?"

"Who shot him?"

"Who do you think shot him?"

"I think it was me."

Chapter 21

Washington Heights, NYC
13 August 2008
12:30 p.m.

They found another body in the building on 187th," Tolya said to Pete standing in the doorway of their office.

"Where? What? When?"

Tolya dropped into his chair. "The Captain just told me as I was coming in. Just now, in the basement on 187th street."

"How? They're working again?"

"Yeah, he cleared them to begin demolition again yesterday. We were out. He says he sent us email."

Pete chuckled. "I don't check my email if I'm not on duty."

"Neither do I, or I'd be on duty all the time. A text would have been a better idea."

"I'm not sure the Cap knows how to text," Pete replied.

Tolya took a deep breath. "Maybe he should learn. We have to go over there right now. Grab your stuff. The CSU is there already."

Perfect summer weather continued. The sky was deep blue and cloudless, the humidity low and the temperature comfortable. It reminded Pete of a February day in Santo Domingo.

The trot to the construction site took less than five minutes. Tolya looked up at the third-floor windows of the Yeshiva on the corner of Broadway and West 186th street. He wondered if Shalom was at his desk watching.

When they hit the hill at West 187th Street Tolya slowed down a bit. Pete kept moving at the same quick pace he had on Broadway. Tolya grinned. Despite the fact that he kept himself in top shape—he and Pete worked out together four, sometimes five days a week—he was always a little jealous of Pete's stamina, his natural athleticism. Pete reached the scene a full ten seconds before he did.

Manny Blake, the chief crime scene investigator, was standing in front of the building. A few years older than Tolya, he had been with the force for about twenty years. About as tall as he and Pete, and in good shape, he had a thick head of reddish hair and a goatee. He always wore the same disappointed expression, made even more so by inquisitive, searching eyes. Precinct legend had it that he had been a brilliant detective. He'd made grade years before his peers. But he couldn't take the pressure. Blake became too involved in both the lives and the deaths of the victims in his cases. After a fifth murder investigation was sent to cold cases, he requested a transfer to CSU and concentrated on the technical elements rather than the psychological. It took a certain thick skin to separate from the victim to solve the crime. That wasn't necessary with evidence and corpses. Blake didn't have that thick skin, at least that's what the gossip said. At times, Tolya wasn't sure he had it either.

"Kurchenko, how are you," Blake said, extending his hand.

"Good. Wasn't expecting this first thing in the morning. What we got?"

Blake looked at his clipboard, took in a deep breath and let it out slowly. "Not much, a skeleton and the shreds of some clothes, the remains of a wallet."

"Was there anything in the wallet?" Tolya asked.

Blake handed rubber gloves to both Pete and Tolya. He carefully took the remains of a leather wallet from a plastic evidence bag and gently unfolded it. There was a faded driver's license in the billfold.

"Can we take that out?" asked Pete.

Blake hesitated a moment. His bushy eyebrows, the color of a copper penny, hiked up into his forehead. Both Pete and Tolya knew he was a stickler for procedure. "Generally, I wouldn't permit this, but considering how long this body has likely been here, and how unlikely it is the killer will be caught, go ahead."

Tolya gingerly slipped the delicate yellowed paper from the pocket of the leather wallet with the tweezer Blake had handed him. He was concerned that either the paper would tear, or the leather would disintegrate, or both. "Is there any chance of pulling a usable print from the wallet?" he said before he freed the license from its tomb.

Blake smiled and shook his head. "Not a chance."

Tolya let out his breath. He and Pete examined the fragile, flimsy paper as it fluttered in the morning breeze, staring at the name. The type was badly faded. "Can you make it out?" Tolya asked.

"I think so," said Pete, squinting. "It looks like…Eduardo Sanchez."

Tolya stared at the washed-out letters. He could clearly make out Eduardo, though the "u a and r" were significantly more faded than the "Ed" and the "do." The Sanchez faded out at the "ch" and the "ez" was gone completely, a hole blotting out the paper where the final letters would be. "You're sure?"

"It kinda makes sense, bro," Pete replied. The first name is definitely Eduardo, the most likely Spanish surname that would fit here would be Sanchez. It's pretty common."

"Why are you assuming the victim is Hispanic?" asked Blake.

"Because the last body we found here was identified as a Dominican immigrant and the owners of the property at that time had also lived in the Dominican Republic," said Pete.

"Interesting," replied Blake.

"How did you find the body?" Tolya asked.

"The workmen were clearing out some old junk," Blake said, pointing to a rusted washing machine and some old, battleship-gray, filing cabinets now resting on the curb about ten feet away. "They went to break up the floor, it was a dirt floor if you can believe that, but packed down so tight it required a jackhammer, and lo and behold they came upon some bones. Wanna take a look?"

"Sure," they both said.

They followed Blake into what remained of the old house and down the ancient, creaky, wooden stairs into the basement. The workmen had strung up some lights. Toward the back of the room was some police tape separating off the area where the skeleton was found.

"Pretty creepy, no?" said Blake.

"Very creepy, yes," replied Tolya.

Tolya looked at the bones still partially covered by packed earth. "How contaminated is the scene?"

"Very."

"Will you be able to determine much?"

"Not sure," said Blake. "We do what we can. Considering what was already found upstairs, it looks like we might have a serial killer here."

Pete glanced at Tolya. Both knew that intrinsically that wasn't the case.

❧❧❧

Tolya felt his stomach turn as Anisa wheeled Erno into the living room. He liked the old man. Over the years since Max Rothman's murder he had developed a kind of friendship with him. They were in a way, kindred spirits. Tolya rarely opened up about his feelings with anyone other than Pete. He didn't trust people enough for that. Erno, on the other hand, was like a kind, old, uncle. He had the ability to listen and rarely criticized. Instead he guided, and he understood Tolya's conflicts, because though their experiences were separated by half a century, they were similar enough for Erno to understand what Tolya was feeling. Tolya wanted to give Erno peace in what were clearly the final days of his life. This investigation was preventing that. Perhaps Karin was right. Why not just close the case? Four decades had passed. That past was most certainly by now ancient history.

"You woke me from my nap, gentlemen," Erno said, smiling weakly. He pulled the wool shawl over his shoulders more tightly.

"We're sorry to bother you again," Tolya said. He glanced at Pete.

"Does the name Eduardo Sanchez mean anything to you?"

Erno's face remained blank. "No, why?"

"We found his body buried in the basement at your old rooming house," said Tolya.

Erno closed his mouth and pressed his lips together then nodded almost imperceptibly. "I see. That may explain some things I've wondered about for many years."

"What things?"

"In the weeks that followed Vargas' death," Erno said, "Max was very depressed and very tense. Then suddenly his demeanor changed and one day I found him whistling on the porch. He told me it was over, and he never wanted to speak of any of it again."

"You didn't kill this Sanchez guy and you didn't know anything about it?" Tolya asked, interrupting.

"No, I didn't kill him, and in all probability his name wasn't Eduardo Sanchez."

"Then who did?" Pete asked.

Erno lifted his head and took a deep breath, causing his body to shudder. "Being the gambler that I was, I would have to say Max." Erno smiled and coughed. "Imagine, he never told me about it. I had no idea till now."

"Is there anything else you can tell us?" Pete asked.

"No," Erno shook his head, staring off past Tolya and Pete into the hallway, the photos of him and Max, Ava and Helen, half in shadow. "Nothing, really."

"Why do you say his name probably wasn't Eduardo Sanchez," asked Tolya?

"For the same reason Vargas' name wasn't Vargas. He was a friend of Vargas, he got out of Santo Domingo the same way at the same time, and I'm sure he had help too. All those fascist bastards did. When they got here, they tried to hide, new identities, new lives, until they thought they could return to Santo Domingo, until one of Trujillo's sons or his deputies took back power."

"Do you have any idea who this guy was?"

"If I'm right about who I think he was, about my memories, he was a friend of Vargas. We ran into him once at a Yankee's Stadium."

"Who was there?"

"Max, me, and Stephen."

"Rabbi Rothman knew him?" Tolya asked. He glanced at Pete. Pete's raised eyebrow indicated he knew exactly what Tolya was thinking and where he was going with this line of questioning.

"Stephen?" Tolya asked.

"Yes, Max's son? Or Rabbi Rothman, as you call him, No." Erno laughed, "Stephen didn't know either of them. He had met Vargas at the rooming house. He was with us at the ballgame. We took him, he was a boy. We ran into them, an accident, a coincidence, whatever you'd like to call it. I doubt Stephen would even remember it."

"Erno," Tolya said, "What are you telling us?" He feigned confusion, hoping to get more information.

"It's simple," Erno said. His voice so soft they had to lean in to hear him. "Vargas saw us at Yankee Stadium. He was with another man. They came over to where we were sitting. I saw Max's expression when he caught sight of the man. I knew he knew him and assumed why."

"Did you ask Max who this guy was?" Pete said.

"Yes, but at first he wouldn't tell me. Later he did."

"What did he say?" Tolya pressed.

"He was there. Max told me this man was there when the man you call Vargas attacked him. I knew. I didn't have to ask. I knew what he was talking about. That guy was one of Vargas' henchmen from that night when José, Nereida, and Anabela were murdered. You know what I'm talking about?"

"Yes, I read about it in Max's diaries," Tolya replied. "Did Max go after him?"

Erno hesitated for a moment. "No, I would doubt that, but I can't say for sure. We were together almost all the time. This guy probably came around the rooming house looking for Vargas after we made him disappear. My guess is Max got scared and killed him. And so, he extracted his revenge. Seems he buried him in the basement and never told me."

Tolya and Pete saw the tears slip from Erno's ancient eyes. This was too much. It was cruel. Tolya's heart sank. How could they continue to do this to an old man? What little time he had left shouldn't be spent remembering the worst moments in his life.

"If I had known what would happen," Erno said through his tears., "I never would have told Max that I had seen Vargas in the first place. Max was my friend, my brother. I ached for him. I wanted him to have some feeling of closure. He saw only hate and anger. It drove him to kill. It seems revenge is sometimes more important for the soul than forgiveness."

"But you said you killed Vargas," Pete said.

Erno took a deep breath that made his entire body shake. He stuck out his chin proudly. "I did. But I didn't kill this Sanchez, or whoever he was."

୧୬୧

Shalom waited patiently in the tiny room with no windows in the ground floor office of Dr. Leah Zimmerman at 400 Central Park West. She came well recommended from Morty, his childhood friend. Like Shalom, Mordy had become *baal t'shuva* during college. Unlike Shalom, Morty had become disillusioned with the committed life. He had left the rabbinate and become a psychologist. Both Shalom and Morty had agreed that Morty shouldn't treat him. He recommended Dr. Zimmerman. She would be sympathetic to Shalom's world view. Though more liberal in her religious outlook now, she had been raised in Orthodoxy.

The door leading to her office opened. A tall, thin woman in modest clothing opened the door. She wore a skirt which ended below her knee, and a long-sleeved, cream-colored blouse buttoned to her neck. She appeared to be around forty-five years old. Her chestnut hair was her own, no wig covered it and broke on her shoulders. She smiled. "Rabbi Rothman I presume?" Shalom rose and smiled back at her. She didn't offer her hand and neither did he, which made him feel comfortable immediately.

"Yes. Nice to meet you too. Thanks for seeing me on such short notice."

"Morty is an old friend and he said there is some level of urgency."

Shalom felt a mild sense of embarrassment. He hoped he hadn't blushed. "Yes, well…"

"Come in." She gestured toward the office beyond the doorway.

Shalom entered the tiny space. He had expected something larger. A desk sat catty-corner partially under the one window, which was obscured with hanging plants. On the opposite wall was a recliner. He had pictured a couch, though none would have fit here. Next to the door through which he had entered was a second door designated with the word exit. That would explain how the previous patient had left the room without passing through the waiting room.

"Please, sit there," Zimmerman said, gesturing to the recliner.

Shalom slipped nervously into the chair, settling his thin frame into the corner of one side. He removed his hat, revealing his large, black velvet skullcap. The doctor smiled. "You can put your hat there, on the table next to the lamp." She had a calm, pleasing tone, which, coupled with her smile, made Shalom feel she was trustworthy and empathic. He laughed to himself and smiled back at her. There were reasons people chose specific professions. She appeared very "therapist-ish."

"Why don't you push back on the chair and put your legs up. Relax a bit," Dr. Zimmerman said.

Shalom felt a bit uncomfortable about reclining in front of a woman. "No, I'm fine thanks." He placed his hat on his lap.

"What brings you here, Rabbi?"

Shalom looked about the room before speaking. The doctor's degrees were on the wall behind her. He considered leaving, then stopped himself. "Do you believe, doctor, that the mind can change or re-write events?"

"Why do you ask?"

"Because I'm not sure."

"Why are you unsure?"

"Because I am a man of faith. I believe *HaShem* guides us. He helps us to choose between good and evil. We can choose the wrong path, but then we have memory. Even when we choose the wrong path *HaShem* is there to help us to repent, to make *t'shuvah*."

The doctor smiled. "I haven't heard anyone use those terms with such genuine affection and conviction in many years. My father believed that."

"Do you believe that?"

"What I believe isn't important. I'm here to help guide you through your confusion. So, to answer your initial question, yes, I do believe the human mind can reconstruct events in ways to help us accept our mistakes and keep our sanity at the same time. What do you believe your mind is hiding?"

Shalom hesitated. His stomach twisted. He had never discussed this with another human being, not even Rachel. "I think I may have killed someone?"

The doctor didn't flinch. She maintained the same smiling composure she had before Shalom had permitted his deepest, most dreaded thought to escape his mouth.

"If that's the case Rabbi, we have much work to do. Please make yourself comfortable. We still have forty-five minutes."

Chapter 22

Washington Heights, NYC
14 August 2008
10:00 a.m.

P rofessor," said Tolya, "can you explain to us what's in this diary? He and Pete sat uncomfortably on hard wood chairs in Professor Dvorak's office, much smaller than the offices of either Professor Tejada or Professor Anderson. But then this professor was only an assistant professor.

"I can give you a picture of what's in here though I haven't finished reading it yet, let alone translating the entire thing. It's one of the oddest documents I've ever read."

"Why so?" asked Pete.

"Well, first of all, I've never seen a diary that wasn't in chronological order."

"Can you explain?" Tolya said.

"It's as if after the first entry, which is the earliest entry, he randomly picked spots to jot down thoughts or stories and gave no thought to placing later items on blank pages in between earlier entries."

"I don't understand," Pete said.

"He literally picked up the diary and opened to a blank page and began writing. Then the next time he might put an entry on whatever blank pages were between two earlier entries. Here, let me show you the dates." The professor leaned over the desk and showed them the first entry then flipped to several others he had marked with yellow post-it notes. "You see, there are entries from 1948, after entries from 1964."

"Why would he do that?" Tolya asked.

"I have no idea, I didn't know the man, but I would venture a guess that he was very agitated when he did it. Also, I haven't come across an entire story. It's as if these are explanatory notes to something he's written elsewhere, and he wants these most private thoughts, which I might add are often very dark, to remain deeply hidden. There seems to be some ultimate truth here designed to purge his soul far away from anyone else's prying eyes."

"Are there any constants or recurring things that might help us?" Pete said.

The professor hesitated for a moment. "I feel as if I'm exposing someone's nakedness."

"The author's been dead a few years, if that helps," Tolya said. "We really need to know what's in there. It pertains to a murder investigation."

Dvorak sighed. "It doesn't really help, but I will tell you anyway." The professor leaned forward, his elbows on his desk, thumbing through the diary's pages. "He considers suicide at least a half-dozen times. He's miserable. He feels life has dealt him an unworkable hand, and perhaps more importantly, that fate is somehow after him."

"Does he talk about god?"

"He muses about God, he questions god's existence. He rails against him a few times. He wonders if he is being punished for his lack of faith or perhaps his ignoble acts."

"Does he say what acts?"

"He refers vaguely to incidents he wrote about elsewhere. Are there other diaries?"

"Yes," replied Tolya.

"Have you read them?"

"Some of them, not all," said Pete.

"I think you need to connect these to their original references."

"Could you translate them for us? As is?"

The professor smiled. "Of course, but I'd have to charge you for translation services, and it might not be only me looking at it. It's good work for grad students. Would you be okay with that?"

Tolya glanced at Pete, that same private half-smile they shared whenever one knew the other's thinking. This professor wanted to shake down the NYPD for a few bucks. "Sure," said Tolya. "But we need this day after tomorrow."

The professor thumbed through the diary and it's small, cursive, old-fashioned lettering. "That's a very short fuse."

"We only want the passages dated from 1965-1966 right now. We can do the rest later. We'll pay double the regular rate."

The professor nodded his head. "Okay, officers, see you day after tomorrow around noon."

Tolya stuck out his hand. "Thanks."

"And that's detectives," added Pete.

附

Shalom signed off on the last of the acceptances for this year's classes and slipped the folder back into his briefcase. He glanced at the ornate, wooden clock, shaped like a seven-pointed starburst on the wall next to the door. Dr. Zimmerman would be coming through it in a few moments. He wasn't entirely sure how he felt about that. A psychologist's office was the last place he'd ever have expected to find himself. When he needed solace or understanding he would seek it in *Torah* or *Talmud,* or the endless commentaries written about both. That wasn't working anymore.

"Good afternoon," Zimmerman said, the door opening, the sunlight from behind her flooding into the room, casting her shadow over Shalom.

Shalom noted the time, she was very prompt. "Good afternoon," he replied.

"Please come in."

Shalom followed the doctor into the office. This time he went directly to the recliner. He placed his hat on the table next to it and pushed back slightly, the footrest lifting his legs.

"Did you take some time to think about what we discussed in our last session?" Zimmerman asked?

Shalom considered her question. He had thought about it, but in the same way he would consider the problem of a congregant, as an unbiased third-party giving guidance, not as a participant in the event.

"Yes," he said, "though I'm not sure I connected to it the way you were hoping. It still feels like I'm thinking about someone else, not me."

"You need to own it, Shalom. That's how we get to the truth."

Shalom breathed deeply. "I understand." He settled back into the recliner

"Do you ever think of your parents as happy?" the Doctor asked, her voice controlled and soothing.

Shalom pictured them both in his mind. Differing images flashed in a stream. There was rarely a smile on both their faces at the same time. "Why?"

Doctor Zimmerman leaned slightly forward. "Remember Rabbi, I ask the questions here." She smiled.

"Of course." He relaxed into the chair. "It's hard for me to say they were happy in the conventional sense. I can remember moments when they smiled, but I can't remember long periods where they seemed happy."

"Were they ever happy at the same time?"

"Rarely."

"Can you tell me one time when they were?"

Shalom thought for a moment. "When I was accepted to college."

"How about when you graduated?"

"No, by then I had turned to religion and my father disapproved."

"Tell me how they reacted when you were accepted at college?"

"They hugged me, both of them. That was unusual for my father. He wasn't physically demonstrative."

"Why do you think that was?"

"I have no idea."

"Can you tell me of another time when he was physically demonstrative with you?"

This time Shalom didn't hesitate. "Funny, I was thinking about that recently, a few days ago."

"Why?"

"I was thinking about how I behave with my own son."

"Are you demonstrative?"

Shalom averted his eyes from the doctor. "My son doesn't, or should I say, well, he is autistic."

Zimmerman shook her head. "I understand. Do you wish you could be more physically demonstrative with your son? What's his name?"

"Baruch. And yes, I do."

"How beautiful," she said, "your son's name is blessing, and yours, peace."

"Thank you." Shalom felt himself relax a bit. He could trust this doctor. She understood where he was coming from.

"Can you tell me about this other time you remember your father being demonstrative with you?"

"Sure. I was around twelve. We went to a Yankee game with my uncle Erno. He put his arm around me. It stayed like that for several innings."

"What happened to change it?

Shalom tensed. He remembered the moment clearly. "One of my father's tenants showed up with another man, and after that his whole demeanor changed."

"In what way?"

"He became the same morose, angry, person he generally was."

"Why do you think that is?"

"I don't know. He hated this guy. Every time he was around, my father became agitated, angry."

"Do you know why?"

"No."

"Did you ever ask him?"

"No, but he wouldn't have told me, in any case. He never let me near that part of his life."

"What part of his life?"

"Anything that had to do with the time they spent during the war in Santo Domingo or anyone from there."

"Did your father know this man you saw at the ball game from his time there?"

"I assume so, but I don't know for sure."

"Is there anyone you could ask?"

Shalom pushed down the leg rest on the recliner. "I want to, no, I have to, be truthful," he said.

"Yes, you do. For your own sake."

"I asked my uncle Erno once. He isn't really my uncle. He was my father's friend. They were refugees in Sosúa together."

"What did he tell you?"

"He said my father didn't like the man. Then I asked him why. He wouldn't tell me. He said it was better the less I knew. I was twelve years old. I was taught to respect my elders. My uncle said to leave it alone."

"Was that the end of the conversation?"

"No, I asked him why they rented the man a room if he didn't like him. He said they needed to keep the business running, money was money."

"How did you feel about this man?"

"I didn't like him. His name was Vargas. He was a very unsavory character. My mother didn't like him either. She told my father to keep him away from me."

"What did your father do?"

"He said not to worry, he would be gone soon."

"Was he?"

"Yes, not that long thereafter."

"Who was this man, as you remember him? Who was he to your twelve-year-old self?"

Shalom leaned forward in the chair. He felt his lunch inch up his throat. "He's the man I think I killed."

Doctor Zimmerman walked around the desk and pulled a folding chair from against the wall and opened it. She sat close enough to Shalom to be emotionally intimate, to coax the memory out of him, while not touching him, knowing that would set off a reaction that would connect him from the place he had opened to.

"Why do you think you killed him?"

Shalom eyes filled with tears. The doctor reached across to the desk and took two tissues from the box and handed them to Shalom. "That's all right. You can cry without shame here."

Shalom wiped his eyes and then sobbed. "I don't know. It's so confusing."

"What, Shalom. Tell me what you see in your mind. What were you doing there?"

Shalom sat back in the recliner and dried his eyes. He thought back to that night, so long ago, an image in front of his eyes which he had tried to forget so many times. For years he thought he had erased it, then in walked Kurchenko and his partner with that photograph and the whole horrific scene came back at him. He couldn't remember all of it though, only parts, and mostly the blast of the gun going off and the terror of the moments that followed.

"I was walking home from Morty's house. He lived up on Audubon Avenue. I was coming down 187th Street and passing the rooming house. There were fireworks still going off. It was the Fourth of July. Morty and I had gone to see some fireworks over in Highbridge Park. I could hear shouting coming from inside, my father's voice, uncle Erno, another voice."

"Whose voice?"

"That man, Vargas."

"What did you hear?"

Shalom stared at the cracks in the paint on the ceiling. He dragged his memories out from deep inside. "Vargas was threatening my father. *Te mato*, he said. That means I'll kill you, in Spanish." Shalom surprised even himself. He generally refused to speak a word of Spanish. People were surprised when they discovered that he spoke the language. "I went up the stairs to the front door quickly. When I got to the top, I flung open the door. It was unlocked. I screamed, 'Pop.' They all turned to me. They were in the dining room. Vargas had a gun. It was pointed at my father." Shalom began to shake. He thought he might vomit.

He grabbed the arm of the chair. "I don't know if I can continue."

"Take a breath."

Shalom shuddered. "I didn't know what to do."

"What were they saying?"

"I'm not sure. My father was talking about his friend José and someone else, shouting at Vargas."

"Do you remember the other person's name?"

"I always thought it was Anabela or something like that. I wasn't familiar with the name."

"Then what happened?"

"Then I remember the sound and the flash of the gunshot."

"Did your father have a gun?"

"No, I asked my Uncle recently, before I began seeing you, he said only Vargas had one, that Vargas misfired and that he grabbed the gun himself and shot Vargas."

"And what do you remember after that?"

Shalom saw and heard the skirmish rattling around in his head as if it were happening now. "My father screaming, 'what have you done, you have ruined me again,' then nothing, only that my uncle grabbed me and the next thing I remember he is in my room with me at home. He tells me that my father is fine and that we can never speak of this again, especially not to my mother or Aunt Ava, his wife."

"Where was your father?"

"I'm not sure."

"Did you ever speak to him of the incident again, or to anyone?"

"The next day. My father said that for his sake I must never say a word to anyone. That he and uncle Erno could end up in prison and that he loved me. That both of them loved me."

"What did you do?"

"I did as I was told." Shalom felt the beads of sweat slipping behind his collar and down his back. "I've spent years erasing that night from my mind."

⌘

"So where are you at, gentlemen?" the Captain asked. "We need to wrap this up. We have real cases involving recent events."

Tolya looked over at Pete. "We're making progress. We should have a better insight day after tomorrow."

"What happens day after tomorrow?"

"We'll have the translations from Rothman's last diary."

"We think it will fill in the holes," added Pete.

"I think I need to understand this a little more than I do," said the Captain.

"We believe what's in there will tell us who killed Vargas…" said Tolya.

"…And by extension, Sanchez," said Pete.

The Captain sat back in his chair, the rim of its back scraping against the wall. "I thought we had a confession. The old man killed Vargas and then he told you the dead guy killed Sanchez. Jeez, what are we snooping around here for?"

"The truth," said Tolya.

"The truth?" shouted the Captain, catapulting out of his chair, his stomach bouncing up and down as his palms landed on the desk. "At this point, does it really matter? We aren't going to prosecute anyone. Did you see the report from Blake?" He pulled the CSU report from the middle of a pile of papers on the left side of his desk and slapped it down in front of Pete and Tolya. "Conclusive," he shouted. "There were a number of stab marks on the ribcage and skull that indicated that the victim was attacked with a hammer head and a knife-like object. They count at least twelve. The guy was hacked to death almost forty years ago. What's the problem? We've got plenty to attend to in the here and now!"

"Okay, Captain," said Tolya. "We get it. Close the case. We just need two more days. Thirty-six hours really. Let's just see it through."

"Why?"

"Because we owe the dead that much," said Tolya. And, he thought, the living as well.

Chapter 23

Washington Heights, NYC
15 August 2008
10:00 a.m.

Tolya and Pete were surprised when they received the call earlier that morning from Professor Tejada. His parents were willing to talk about his uncle, Vicente Tejada, a/k/a, Fernando Vargas.

Pete knocked gently on Tejada's outer office door then opened it. The professor's secretary was behind her desk, same as last time, but this time Pete got a smile.

"Oh, hello detectives. Come right in," she said. "He's, I mean they're, expecting you." Pete poked Tolya in the side as they walked past the young woman and into the professor's office. Tolya wouldn't give Pete the satisfaction of acknowledging it.

"Good morning," Tejada said, his small, wiry, frame emerging from behind his desk. He gestured to a couple in their seventies siting to his right on folding chairs. "These are my parents, Hilda and Armando Tejada. Please sit down."

"I want to thank you for agreeing to see us," said Tolya. "Would you prefer to conduct this interview in English or Spanish?"

"English is fine," said Armando Tejada.

"That works for us too," said Pete.

Pete and Tolya settled into chairs opposite them. Tolya took out a pad and pen, and a small device. "Do you mind if we record this?"

Hilda Tejada glanced at her husband. "No, that's alright," she said taking a tentative breath.

"What made you come forward now?" asked Tolya, turning on the recorder.

Armando looked at Hilda before answering. She nodded. "After so many years we felt it was the time for the truth," he said. "We were very ashamed of my uncles. They did terrible things."

"What kind of things?" asked Pete.

Hilda took Armando's hand. "Vicente in particular was a murderer and a rapist."

"Here?" Tolya questioned.

"No, in Santo Domingo."

"How do you know this?" Tolya continued.

"When we were children, really until we were almost twenty, Trujillo ruled the island. My father worked for him in some respect, you know they gave him a job at a factory he owned. He got that job because my uncles…"

"Uncles? More than one?" asked Pete. He glanced at Tolya

"Yes, my uncles, Vicente and Raphael, worked for Trujillo directly. They were officially in the police station, but mostly they did his dirty work."

"What exactly does that mean?" said Tolya.

"They intimidated people, they procured women for Trujillo. When they were told to, they made someone disappear. For this they were paid money, and given houses, and their families were taken care of. So, as I said, my father, their brother, got a job."

"Did you know about this when you lived in Santo Domingo," asked Pete. He felt a shiver run down his spine. He wondered how much his own grandfather knew, and what he did in those days. Pete knew he too had been given a job for life.

Pete worshiped his *abuelo*, this larger than life figure, always with a fedora or his Licey cap perched on his head, his huge arms open and welcoming whenever Pete visited. He was perennially happy the way most Dominican men are, rarely if ever permitting the world to see the deep disappointments and betrayals of their own lives.

"We didn't talk about such things," Armando Tejada said, his eyes focused on the carpet under his feet.

"But you knew he did these things?" Tolya continued.

"Everyone knew."

"How?"

Hilda put a hand on Armando's arm to stop him. She picked up the story, her tone both angry and defiant. "First of all, he bragged about it when he was drunk, which was pretty much every night, how he would hunt for young girls for Trujillo, how he had settled scores for him, and how he had been paid with the land or daughters of those who had been punished. And I was to be one of those prizes."

The impact of that statement wasn't lost on anyone in the room. Eventually, the poison would kill even the snakes who carried it. Professor Tejada rose from his chair and walked to the window, his back to Tolya, Pete, and his parents. He attempted to stifle his sobs but couldn't. It felt as if the shame of an entire people had descended into this one room, a continent away, a half century later.

Pete was caught speechless. This was the same world he and his family had come from. The stories were true, despite those who claimed convenient amnesia. One man had terrorized a nation for more than thirty years, and the scars of those times were still open.

Hilda rose from her seat and went to her son. She put her hand over his shoulder and led him back to his chair, her strength both surprising and evident. "There's more *mijo*, and you need to know. I'm sorry we never told you, you deserved to know."

Tolya was uncertain what to do. He was uncomfortable witnessing this family's secrets exposed to the light of day in front of him. The naked truth was uncovering more than just Erno's and Max's secrets now. He could never have talked about his family's confidences in this public of a way, about their tragedies and shames, of how his mother had offered herself in front of him to a bureaucrat with the power to save his brother's life. "Are you sure you want to continue, *señora*?" he asked.

"*Sí*, it's time the truth was told." Hilda Tejada settled herself back into her chair, her back straight as a board, her chin proudly thrust forward. "I was engaged to Armando. We were students and we were fortunate. Both of our families were involved to some extent with the dictatorship. In those days, you accepted that. It bought you a seat at

University, it gave you privileges. Santo Domingo was a very poor country. We looked away from the crimes of the government if they weren't against us. Armando and I were a little different from others we knew though. It was at the time when the Mirabel sisters stood up to Trujillo that we started to understand what we needed to do. We became part of the secret resistance."

"We met at the University. We fell in love. We were engaged to be married when we finished school. Trujillo spied me at a lunch that my parents were invited to in Puerto Plata. He sent down orders that I was to come to meet him a few days later. Everyone knew what that meant. My father was terrified. There was nothing he could do. If he tried to stop it, he would end up in jail or worse. Vicente was ordered to bring me to him. He sent Raphael to warn us."

"Raphael is?" asked Pete.

"My other uncle, Vicente's brother," said Professor Tejada.

Pete looked over at Tolya. "I think that might be Sanchez."

"I think you may be right." Tolya focused on Hilda Tejada, the butterflies in his stomach building. "*Señora*, did Raphael ever come here?"

"*Sí*, shortly after Vicente. We refused to see him." Hilda Tejada, clutched her bag to her body. "He was even worse than Vicente. He leered at me whenever he came around. I was terrified of him." She choked up on that last statement, then calmed herself.

"What did you do after you were warned that Trujillo had asked for you?" the Professor asked his mother.

Hilda began to weep. Armando put his arms around her. *"Ta bien mi amor. Le digas la verdad."*

She looked at her son and sighed. "I'm sorry we lied to you all these years." She pulled a handkerchief from her bag and wiped her eyes, straightened up, and continued. "Vicente had a plan. He was a double agent. He worked for the Americans as well, spying on Trujillo. He contacted them. My father, my mother, my two sisters and me, we were taken that night out of the country. We went first to Haiti and then to Miami. My father was declared a traitor and everything we owned was confiscated. Trujillo took everything."

"But I don't understand, didn't Trujillo's people wonder how you found out?" Pete asked.

"Vicente and Raphael covered that." Hilda shivered. "They went to a brothel in Puerto Plata and found a young girl about my height, weight and color, and took her out for the night. They got her very drunk then they beat her to death." As she said this her composure broke. "She died for me, that poor girl." Hilda crossed herself. "May God forgive me."

Tolya looked at Pete. "I don't get it."

Pete couldn't speak. He was near to retching his breakfast.

"They killed another young girl in place of you." Professor Tejada said, almost inaudibly.

Hilda Tejada continued the explanation. "They delivered this young girl's body to Trujillo and told him she was me. They told him they killed her because she had refused to come willingly. That only served to reassure him of their allegiance because he believed they killed their nephew's fiancé." Hilda gagged. She covered her mouth and turned her head.

"That wasn't unusual," said Armando, his arm over Hilda's shoulder, attempting to comfort her. "If a young girl said no, they would kill her parents, or a sister, or brother, or beat her. In this case, my uncles told Trujillo that when they arrived my wife's father refused to send her, so they beat him, grabbed her, and left him there, and that he must have fled. Then on the way to Trujillo's residence in Puerto Plata, they said she tried to escape, and they caught her and beat her too, and that she died from the beating."

"And Trujillo didn't care that they killed her rather than deliver her?" Tolya said.

"No, he just moved on to the next virgin. He prized loyalty over anything else."

Tolya rose from the chair and walked to the window. Even the horrors of Soviet internal exile didn't come near this. "Did you want to take a break?" he asked, more for himself than for them. I still have more questions."

Hilda and Armando looked at each other. "No," she said. "After today I never want to speak of this again. Let's finish."

"Okay, well, I have to tell you that I do. I'm gonna need about an hour and a stiff drink before I can continue, if that's all right with you," said Tolya.

"Me too," said Pete.

By the time they reconvened Tolya had calmed himself down. Terror was terror, whether it was the Soviet Union or Trujillo's Dominican Republic. Their story had sickened him to a point where he couldn't control his thoughts. He had banished the demons from his mind with the help of a single malt scotch at 11:00 in the morning.

"Can you explain how your uncles came to New York?" Tolya asked.

Armando straightened in the chair and began. "After Trujillo was assassinated the people began to look for the men who had enforced his rule. My uncles had made no secret of what they did. As Hilda said, when they were drunk, which was every night, they had big mouths. In nineteen-sixty-five, my uncles were sort of in hiding in the Capital. Less people knew them there than in Puerto Plata. Also, Vicente had changed his name and had himself declared dead. He called himself Fernando Vargas. Then someone spotted him, and people started to come around looking for him at night. He lived with his sister—my aunt—and her husband in the old part of the Capital. As I told you, Vicente also worked for the Americans, so he contacted them, and they arranged to bring him here for a new life. Raphael didn't have those contacts, but Vicente made a deal to bring him here too, a month later."

"When did they come?" asked Pete.

"It was in nineteen-sixty-five around Christmas and Raphael a little while later. I remember it was cold and they didn't want to come out of the house."

"When Vicente showed up at my parent's house I nearly fainted," said Hilda. "Yes, in a way he saved my life, but he was a rapist and murderer, nonetheless. I told my father I wouldn't stay in the same house with him. My father said he had no choice because of what Vicente had done to help us. Armando was living in a rooming house in Washington Heights. I threatened to go to live with him. My father couldn't permit that, so I relented. My father got Vicente a job at a Cuban Restaurant on the West Side and helped him to find a room near his work."

"I saw him a few months later walking on Saint Nicholas Avenue," said Armando. "He said he had a girlfriend, a Puerto Rican woman. He was very proud of that. He said he was living in the neighborhood in a boarding house. He wanted us to go have a drink, to catch up. He wanted me to let my father-in-law know he was well. I didn't want to go, but I had no choice."

"Did he mention anything about the place where he rented his room? About the people who ran the boarding house?" Tolya asked.

Armando sighed heavily. "He did, but at the time I didn't pay much attention. After a few drinks he was, how do you say, loose, like always when he drank. He told me how he was renting a room from two Jews from Sosúa, and that the funny part for him was that he knew them. As a matter of fact, he said, he had killed the girlfriend of one of them and thought he had killed the Jew as well, but he must have nine lives like a cat, because the Jew was alive and breathing. He laughed like a madman and said he wasn't done with them. He was trying to figure out a way to kill them and steal the rooming house business from them."

Pete and Tolya looked at each other. One couldn't make this stuff up. "And you didn't think to go to the police?" Pete asked.

"No. First of all, I didn't know how much to believe. Second, he was my uncle and had saved Hilda's life. Third, I was afraid of the police. They wouldn't listen to a 'spic' like me."

That struck Pete like a knife. Little had changed. Even now, forty some odd years later, many Latinos still didn't trust the police.

"And when he suddenly disappeared?" said Tolya. You didn't look for him?"

"Would you?" said Armando.

"And when Raphael disappeared?"

"We figured he was with Vicente. They were always together anyway." Armando and Hilda stood up. They turned to their son. "I'm sorry *mijo*, we should have told you everything, we should have told you the truth a long time ago, but we wanted you to be proud of your heritage. Santo Domingo is so much more than Trujillo and his henchmen."

"I know that, papa," the Professor said. He flung his arms around them both, embracing them tightly. Tolya and Pete heard a litany of "*te amo*" and "*lo siento*" and "*disculpa me*." They quietly exited the room, leaving the Tejadas to come to their own peace with their past.

Chapter 24

Washington Heights, NYC
15 August 2008
4:00 p.m.

It took a full day for Shalom to compose himself sufficiently before visiting Erno again. He had to have answers. Burying the past deep in his mind, both known and suspected, was no longer an option. Erno was waiting for him in the living room when he arrived. He promised himself he would remain calm. He wanted the truth, but he also realized Erno's advanced age represented two danger points; if he didn't ask for the truth soon, he might not have the chance, and if he pushed too hard, he could endanger the life of an old man.

"You're back, Stephen," Erno said.

Shalom breathed deeply to control himself. Though he disliked being addressed by his secular name, he tolerated it from Erno. "I need to understand some things."

"What, *mijo*?" Erno asked.

The use of the term *mijo*, a Spanish endearment for my son, reminded Shalom of his father. It was what his father called him when he let the wall down between them, when he reached out. He suspected Erno meant to disarm him emotionally by using it.

"Who was Anabela?"

Erno's expression changed with the mention of the name. It was as if a cloud covered him. "Why? What difference does it make now?"

"Because I am beginning to remember. I'm seeing a therapist…"

Erno smiled. His chest rose as if to laugh, but the energy required from his body wasn't there. "A therapist. I see. And what have you remembered?"

"I was there, in the room, my father shouted that name."

"It was a long time ago and I don't remember."

Shalom hesitated. It went against his nature, who he was, to pressure a person this way. Yet, he had to know. "Erno-*bacsi*," he said, "please."

Erno peered off into the darkness of the hallway that lead to the front of the apartment. "I suppose it's time you knew everything." He hesitated for one moment then looked Shalom directly in his eyes. Shalom thought he saw a tear in Erno's. "I'm sorry Stephen, I lied to you when you were here last. I had to consider what your father and mother wanted kept private. Here is the truth. She was your father's lover. She was to become his wife. She was pregnant with his child when she was murdered. She was the woman Trujillo sent his henchman for."

Hearing this knocked the air from Shalom's lungs. He took a moment to collect himself. "That's why he left my mother? He left her alone in that jungle to live with a Dominican woman?"

Erno smiled. "It's funny how we never suspect our mothers of bad behavior," Erno said, his voice displaying a strength even he was surprised by.

"What are you saying?" Shalom felt as if his head would explode. As a teenager he was both embarrassed and angered by the way his father flirted with woman, even in front of his mother, but this, this was something much worse. He'd abandoned his mother for another woman. "He never ceases to disgust me, even dead," Shalom shouted.

"Your parents were the victims of many poor decisions and turns of fate." Erno replied, his voice louder than he could remember it being in years. "Did you know that their marriage was arranged?"

"No." Shalom caught himself, checked his anger. He sat back down, ashamed that he'd shouted at an old man.

"Do you think they would have left Europe if not for Hitler?" Erno continued.

Shalom didn't have to answer.

"They were miserable with their situation and with each other."

Shalom felt the tears begin to slide from his eyes down to his cheeks and into his beard. Why hadn't his parents trusted him with this? He would have loved them regardless.

"As I told you the last time you were here, after the baby was lost, we brought them back to Sosúa. They didn't speak to each other for months. Your mother blamed your father for everything, and he deserved the blame, but he did a fine job at inflicting even more pain on himself."

Shalom saw the fire burning in Erno's eyes.

"Your father begged her to forgive him, but she wouldn't. Your mother even took up with another refugee. Surprised?" Erno chuckled. "His name was Fritzy. A German. Are you still so shocked that your father left the settlement and took up with a Dominican woman? She made him happy. Happier than I'd ever seen him."

"What happened to her?" Shalom asked, the words barely audible.

"She was the one murdered by Trujillo's men. Trujillo saw her at a cotillion in Puerto Plata and wanted her for himself. She was pregnant with your father's child. That bastard Tejada and his henchmen came to José's village to abduct Anabela. He and his men killed her, José and José's wife, and left your father for dead. Your father had his revenge."

Shalom was speechless. Finally, he said, "I'm sorry, Erno-*bacsi*. Forgive me. I shouldn't cause you to relive this pain."

Erno lifted his bony finger to his cheek to wipe away the tears that fell silently from his ancient eyes. "No need to apologize. You should have known the truth long ago, at least some of it. But it was theirs to tell you, not mine. A man's marriage should remain between him and his wife. Nonetheless, you need to know that your parents loved you, both of them, and believe it or not they loved each other."

"That leaves one question," Shalom said, unable to look at Erno.

"And that would be?"

"Did I shoot Vargas?"

ᘓᘐᘓ

Erno settled into the old mattress. Over the years it had molded to his body. Anisa was constantly after him to replace it. He laughed. He would be dead soon. Why would he waste money on such a thing? And besides, he had shared this mattress with Ava. At times he felt as if he could reach out and she would still be there. Despite his philandering, he loved her still, like no other woman he had ever known. He would have died long ago in Budapest if not for her. Her cunning and her beauty, and yes, her love for him had gotten them out of Budapest. It was a tale no one would ever know. Unlike Max, he had never written it down. It lived in his heart and would die with him.

His visit with Stephen the day before was beyond troubling. He wasn't able to sleep the previous night. He hoped sleep would come to him now, so tired that he felt he was in twilight between reality and fantasy. The conversation had brought back too much. How could someone like Stephen ever understand not only what they had been through, but also what they had done for his sake. If Max could have changed one tiny thing where it concerned Stephen and him, he would have.

Yes, he screamed Anabela's name that night, but he had also howled Stephen's. That was something Stephen hadn't yet remembered. He had howled like a wounded animal, imploring god to lift the curse he believed he carried for his sins, despite his insistence that he didn't believe in god, any god, not the god of his fathers or the gods of others. He had howled Stephen's name too, but Stephen hadn't recovered that part of the memory.

Erno had done as Max asked that night. He tried to calm Stephen down. Stephen was hysterical. Eventually, Erno had no choice, the screaming would attract attention, the sounds from the fireworks beginning to subside. He slapped Stephen across the face twice. Stephen sucked air into his lungs, causing his body to shudder then cough uncontrollably. He hyperventilated then passed out. Erno slung him over his shoulder and slipped out the front door down the hill toward Broadway. For the most part people were too drunk or too engaged to notice him. When one man asked him if he needed help, if everything was all right, he told him his nephew had a few too many beers, waved and continued at a trot up the shallow hill from Broadway to Bennett Ave.

At Bennett, he made a left and walked in the shadows to number 105. He took the service entrance to avoid anyone who might be in the lobby, then the stairs to the third floor. By the time he reached Max's apartment he was out of breath but still able to do what needed to be done. Stephen was heavy, but no heavier than the loads they dragged through the jungle to build Sosúa. The only difference was that Erno was older.

Once inside he brought Stephen to his room and undressed him down to his underwear. He turned on the fan in the window and laid the boy down on the bed. He went into the bathroom and ran the cold water, soaking two towels. He left them in the sink for a moment and went to the kitchen. In the freezer, he found some ice, which he put in a bowl with some water and brought everything to Stephen's room. First, he placed the smaller towel on

Stephen's forehead, then wiped down his arms and legs with the other. He repeated the process with the ice water. After a third time Stephen began to come to.

At first the boy was unaware of where he was. He began to panic. Erno remembered clearly. He had to hold him to the bed. "You're fine, you're in your room," he whispered into his ear. Uncle Erno has you." He embraced the boy. Had he been his own he couldn't have loved him more or felt more pity for him. Stephen was as much a victim of Max's life as Max.

Then Stephen panicked. "What did I do?" he screamed.

Erno put his hand over Stephen's mouth. You didn't do anything, son. What are you talking about?"

"That man, Vargas, is he dead? The blood, all that blood." Stephen began to shake uncontrollably.

"It's nothing, it's nothing, Stephen, calm down. You don't understand what you saw. Everything is fine."

"No, it's not, uncle," Stephen said. He pushed Erno away, wrapping his arms around his torso, shaking. "I'm so cold."

It was over 90 degrees. Erno wasn't sure what to do. He pulled back the light summer blanket from the bed and wrapped it around Stephen. Stephen's eyes stared into the darkness focused on something that wasn't in the room. "Oh, no," he mumbled through shivering lips.

Erno reached into his pocket. He pulled out the small vial of pills he carried with him always, the pills the doctor had given him to fight the panic he would experience from time to time when something reminded him of that moment in Budapest when the fascists had come for them in the elegant apartment he had inherited from his parents.

He was alone when they arrived, Ava had gone to have her hair done, they were to go to the opera that night. He was expecting a delivery from the jeweler, a trinket he had bought to surprise Ava. When he heard the knock he shouted, "the door is open, let yourself in." The next thing he knew he was tied to a chair in the kitchen, a gag in his mouth. The two Iron Guardsman had stripped him to his underwear and were beating him. He was not only a communist but a Jew, and they had had enough of both.

They made themselves comfortable with a bottle of cognac he kept in the kitchen cabinet, taking swigs in between punching him in the face, torso, groin. They were having so much fun they hadn't heard Ava come in. She had found the door ajar and knew something was wrong. With incredible stealth, this five-foot-tall, ninety-pound woman in high heels crept into the living room and retrieved Erno's pistol. When he saw her behind the intruders, Erno nearly panicked. She lifted the gun and shot twice, more deftly than he ever could have himself, their heads exploding everywhere. They left Budapest that night.

"Here, take this," Erno said, placing the pill in Stephen's mouth. "Swallow."

Stephen couldn't get the pill down. Erno ran to the kitchen and brought back a glass with some water. The pill had slipped out of Stephen's mouth onto his chest. Erno took another from the bottle. This time, with the help of the water, Stephen was able to swallow it. Erno looked at his watch. It was midnight. The pill usually took about twenty minutes to work. For Stephen, a twelve-year-old boy, it should work faster. He held Stephen close. As the shivering stopped, he lay him back on the pillow and held his hand till Stephen's breathing indicated he was asleep.

The memory exhausted Erno. He wanted to sleep but couldn't. He tried to close his eyes. Slowly, the darkness of his bedroom receded, and he saw Max's smiling face in the sunshine that day so long ago in Sosúa. Max was in a white shirt and pants. They stood at the edge of the beach. José was there with his son, Josécito. Max held Josécito's hand.

"So. you've made your decision then?" Erno said.

"Yes, I'm sure," Max said. "It's best for everyone. Helen needs her space and so do I. She's entitled to a life. I can't give her what she needs. It's better this way."

"I understand," Erno said. "I will miss you. I never had a brother, until you showed up."

"Thank you for saying that. I will miss you too. You will always be a brother to me. We will see each other. I promise. It's only around the bay. You are always welcome. Anabela will be happy for you to stay with us."

Erno laughed to himself. Max. It was like him to wrap his decision in what was good for Helen, but Erno knew the real motivation. He had fallen in love with Anabela in a way he had never fallen in love before. Erno was a city boy, the son of a rich man. He had had his time to break hearts and have his heart broken. Max never had that. Now he had a chance at real love, real happiness, and Erno was happy for him. "I promise, I will come."

They took some photos on the beach that day then Erno walked Max, José and Josécito to the path that lead to their village. He watched as they grew smaller. Before disappearing into the bushes Max turned and waved. "Thank you, brother," he called out.

Erno opened his eyes. In the darkness, he saw Max standing there. Not the old Max with whom he sat in Bennett Park, nor the middle-aged Max with whom he ran the rooming house. It was the young Max, in his white pants and shirt, the one who left him standing on the beach decades ago in what they then didn't know was paradise.

"Hello, brother," Max said.

Erno wasn't sure if Max had spoken in Hungarian, Spanish or English.

"It's time to go."

"Where are we going?" Erno asked.

"Back to paradise."

Erno felt himself rise from the bed. His body felt light, young again. He smiled. He could almost feel the warm breeze and smell the ocean air. "I'm ready," he said.

"Everyone is waiting for you."

Erno saw Ava approaching out of the darkness, smiling. Helen was with her, José and Nereida behind them. With that he took Max's outstretched hand and felt free for the first time in decades.

Chapter 25
Washington Heights, NYC
16 August 2008
10:15 a.m.

Tolya and Pete waited tentatively for Professor Dvorak. His earlier message was clear, he and his students had come across something useful. Tolya looked at his watch repeatedly. He hated lateness.

"*Tranquilo, hermano,*" Pete said, "he's only fifteen minutes late. Maybe there was a delay on the subway."

Tolya exhaled slowly to calm himself. "What do you think he found?"

"Don't know, but let's hope it finally puts all this to rest. I'm ready to move on after that interview with the Tejadas. That was just a little too intense, bro."

"Sorry detectives," Dvorak said, stepping out of the elevator into the hallway. "My class ran over. Graduate seminar. Please come in." The Professor slipped the key into the door that led to the inner office. "Have a seat, I need only a moment." He reached into his briefcase and took out the diary and a folder and placed them on the desk. He slipped off his tweed sport jacket and hung it over the back of his chair before sitting down. "We found two significant passages both from the summer of nineteen-sixty-six. Of course, there's a lot of other very interesting stuff in there as well. The diary gives a very clear picture over time of the author's mental state and…"

"Professor let's concentrate on the two passages," said Tolya, leaning forward, placing one hand on the desk, anxious to get the answers.

"Yes, of course. Your man is a murderer. He confesses."

Tolya looked at Pete and smiled. Pete raised his hand. Tolya slapped it in a hi-five. "I knew it. Erno was covering for Max all along."

"Well," said Professor Dvorak, "not exactly."

"What do you mean?" Pete said.

"The author, Max, as you refer to him, he clearly details the murder of the second man in mid-August, the eighteenth to be exact."

"And the first murder? Vargas?"

"That's less clear."

"Explain," Tolya said.

Professor Dvorak pulled out the manila folder and opened it. He thumbed through the neatly typed pages. "Here it is. It's dated August twenty, nineteen-sixty-six. May I read this to you?"

"Of course," replied Pete.

"I have very mixed emotions," the Professor began. "I have now committed murder." The professor stopped for a moment. "So, you see he clearly admits it. But that statement also implies it's the first time. Permit me to continue."

"Please," said Tolya. The tension in his gut built up again. The answer wasn't as simple as he might have hoped.

"I really had no choice," Dvorak continued. "When Tejada's henchman showed up looking for him, I was both surprised and frightened. I thought we were finished with this weeks ago when we entombed Tejada in the wall. I was wrong. I couldn't take a chance that this would go any farther. If Sanchez…"

Pete raised his hand to Tolya's in a fist bump. "I told you Sanchez was his name."

Dvorak looked at them both, a bit confused.

"Sorry we interrupted you, Professor," said Tolya. "Please continue."

"…If Sanchez, as he calls himself, went back to the police they could re-open the case. I couldn't take a chance on who might be implicated in Tejada's disappearance. It was time to get on with our lives. I had to make him disappear."

Professor Dvorak paused and took a sip of his coffee. Tolya was surprised at how casual he was about the content. "Does he discuss how he executed the murder?" Tolya asked.

"Yes," replied Dvorak. "He writes a bit about his state of mind first though. Did you want to hear that?"

"Sure," Pete replied.

"I would have thought I would feel remorse or sadness at taking a life. Perhaps if the life I had taken hadn't taken so much from me I might have. I wonder if I still have a soul. If I ever had one. With this bastard's death, my revenge is complete. José, Nereida, and my beloved Anabela can at last rest in peace. I thought when Tejada was dead that would be enough, but somewhere lurking in the back of my mind was the thought that his partners in crime, in the murder of my beloved, my best friend, and his wife, were still walking the same earth as their restive souls. I wanted to finish the job but didn't know how. I knew one was here in New York. I didn't want to seek him out, to stalk him like an animal, yet that's exactly what he is, was. Providence brought him to me. I feel no remorse."

Both Tolya and Pete listened intently. "Should I continue?" the professor asked.

"Yes, please," Tolya replied.

"This is where he describes the event," the Professor said. He cleared his throat then continued. "I invited him into the house and asked him to sit down in the parlor. I offered him a cold drink. He declined. Then he asked me what had happened to Vargas. I laughed to myself. He was maintaining the ruse, using Tejada's alias. I told him he had run off and owed us two weeks rent. Sanchez, or whatever his real name was, said that wasn't possible. They were very close, like brothers, Vargas would have contacted him, let him know where he was. I began to panic but calmed myself out of desperation. I had to end this, once and for always. Then I came upon an idea, a solution. I told him Vargas had left one suitcase, and that if he wanted it I had it in the basement. He said yes, he wanted the suitcase and whatever was in it. He followed me into the basement darkness. I told him to wait at the bottom of the stairs while I turned on the lights. I walked behind him and reached for the hammer I knew was sitting on my workbench, a few feet away. With his back to me I swung the hammer, its claws sinking into the bastard's skull. I hit him with it a few more times till I was sure he was at least unconscious. Then I took a knife and stabbed him in the chest and neck, just to make sure he was finished. I felt finally that the souls of my loved ones could rest.

I could feel the blood all over my shirt. When I turned on the lights the blood was everywhere and all over me. I didn't care. In a way, I felt exhilarated. The feeling was different than when Tejada died, perhaps because this time I was the one who did the killing, I finally had my revenge."

"Whoa," said Tolya. "Stop there. Did you hear that Pete?"

"Yeah, he didn't kill Tejada. But we already know that. This confirms it, Erno killed Tejada, the way he told us he did."

"That may not be the case, gentlemen," said the Professor.

"Why?"

"There's a whole other passage from July eighth, that seems to leave the question of who actually committed the first murder in question. Did you want me to read it?"

Tolya looked over at Pete. Pete tipped his head toward the door almost unperceptively. Tolya got the meaning. "No professor. We have some other things to check out and are short on time." Tolya pulled an envelope from his rear pants pocket and handed it to the Professor. "Here's what we owe you. We'll take the files and go over them ourselves. Thanks for everything."

The Professor took the envelope and slid it into the top drawer of his desk. "As you wish," he said, handing the diary and the manila folder with the translations to Tolya. "Good luck."

Shalom felt as if he had been drained of poison. He took a deep breath in a way he hadn't in years. It was as if he was finally able to breathe freely, without fear of being heard by the ghosts around him. He took three tissues from the box on the small mahogany table next to the recliner and wiped his face. It was wet with a combination of tears and perspiration. He pushed back the recliner, the foot stool raising and extending his legs. They felt light.

"Why don't you loosen your tie and rest for a few moments before we continue," said Dr. Zimmerman.

Shalom felt his cell phone vibrate. It was the third time in the past hour. He never received three calls in an hour. For a moment, he was concerned that something had happened to Baruch. He stopped himself. Carlos was completely capable, and he knew in the case of an emergency to text Shalom, not call. It wasn't Rachel either. The prison only allowed her to call on Sundays. He would attend to whatever it was after his session was over. "Yes," he said. "I need a moment to digest what just happened."

"Close your eyes and relax, Rabbi. I will be back in a few moments."

As the doctor left the room Shalom considered what he had just experienced. It was as intense as a moment of deep prayer. With it came the same feelings of exultation and sorrow. It was finally over. He knew the truth. The question was, what would he do with it. He wiped his face again, closed his eyes and took another deep breath. He could easily fall asleep right now.

"Rabbi," Dr. Zimmerman said, returning to the office, "how are you doing?"

"Okay, considering."

"Yes, that was quite a revelation. Tell me what you're feeling."

"Confused and clear headed, at the same time"

"Are you satisfied that your memory is correct and real?"

Shalom hesitated for a moment. His greatest realization was that he knew what he had remembered all along. "Yes. My question is what do I do with it now? What do I do with myself now? In many ways, this changes everything. It changes my entire life."

"Does it really change everything? Are you the same person you were when this memory happened?"

Shalom considered Dr. Zimmerman's question for a moment. It was a very big question. He wanted to answer honestly and genuinely. "No, I'm not. I was a boy of twelve, now I'm I man of fifty-six. I don't live the same kind of life. I don't even go by the same name."

"Then perhaps the place to start is to forgive everyone involved for what happened. Do you think you can do that?"

Shalom smiled. "You would think that after all these years I could forgive my father," he hesitated, "and my mother." Shalom felt himself choke up. He thought he might break down again. He hated to admit it, but his mother was as much a part of this as his father. She covered for his father, she enabled him. She should have demanded more for herself and Shalom from his father. He realized she hadn't had the strength. What life had served up to them both was more than either could bear, and he had become for both, in their own individual ways, the path to the future.

Then he thought of Baruch, and of Rachel, and he knew that Rachel's inability to accept his autism was in fact the same response his parents had had to him. She had invested everything in him, he was her future. When that future fell apart, so did she.

"I think I can try to start to forgive them now. I don't know that I can ever accept what they did without sadness, but I think I have to accept it if I'm ever to move on."

The doctor smiled. "That's a good beginning. And Erno? He played a major role in this. Can you forgive him?"

"I think I understand what he did now. He was trying to protect me. He loved me like his own child, and I've been very unfair to him. He knew my father's demons. He made a choice to shield me from them, and at the same time help my father expel them."

"Very insightful. The sad truth is that for people like your father, and we've studied them extensively, can never be fully expunge their demons. These demons can be silent for forty, fifty years. The victims act as if everything is fine. They live with their hauntings. In your father's case, those demons may have been too strong for him to tame. When you became *ba'al t'shuva*, he may have felt you betrayed him in favor of the demon he believed destroyed his life to begin with."

"My God?"

"Yes."

Shalom nodded in agreement. He thought to sit up but didn't have the strength to push down the foot stool and right the recliner.

"Rabbi, one more question."

"Yes?"

"Can you forgive that twelve-year-old boy?"

Shalom felt his chest tighten. He knew what the doctor meant. Could he forgive himself? He was hardly that boy any longer. That boy died a long time ago, on that July 4th night in 1966, along with Vargas. That boy's body had continued to function but wasn't really alive again till some eight years later, when Stephen consciously became Shalom, when he chose a different path, a different life. Shalom really was *ba'al t'shuva*. He had returned, psychologically and spiritually from the dead, to a life of faith.

"I'm not sure I can forgive myself for some of the things I've said and done since then, though. I cannot forgive myself for the way I treated my father. He was still my father and I was a grown man, a Rabbi, I knew better. I committed a sin, a terrible sin against both *HaShem* and my father, but that twelve-year-old boy wasn't Shalom Rothman. That boy was Stephen Redmond. You're asking me if I can forgive Stephen Redmond then?"

"That's one way to look at it."

"I believe I can forgive him. He wasn't responsible for what happened. He too was a victim."

Dr. Zimmerman smiled. "I believe you are on the road to healing," she said. "Forgiveness will help you travel that road."

Shalom pushed himself up in the recliner. He looked at the clock on the wall behind the doctor. "We've run over by almost an hour."

"That's all right. When I left the room earlier, I called my next appointment and told her to come later. This was more critical."

Shalom stood. He did something that surprised both the doctor and him. He extended his hand to her. "Thank you, doctor. I can never fully express my gratitude for your help."

Dr. Zimmerman took his hand gently and released it quickly. "You probably don't realize this Shalom, but that gesture you just made is what has sustained you all your life. You're adaptable. You can see past formality when substance is what's called for. Good luck to you."

"Thank you," Shalom said, exiting through the second door into the building hallway. He walked out onto Central Park West and pulled his cell phone from his inside pocket. Erno had called four times.

ⓔⓢⓔⓢ

Tolya stood in front of the evidence board he and Pete had set up in their tiny office. He pointed to the two photos in the second row under the picture of Vargas and Erno. "I don't believe it was either of them. Max admits it wasn't him in the diary and I just don't buy Erno's version of events. Too many inconsistencies. He claims he shot Vargas in the upstairs bedroom. We found evidence of the bullet hole in the parlor."

"True," said Pete. "Then who did it? What happened?"

Tolya reached for the photograph pinned to the board under Max and Erno. He removed the photo and re-pinned it above Max's picture.

Pete smiled. "I agree completely."

"But how?"

"He walked in on the whole thing."

"Why?"

"Go back to the translation."

Tolya picked up the page of translation sitting on top of the pile and read Max's words aloud again.

"We plan. We plan and god laughs. How many times I heard that, first as a boy in Hungary. My mother would say it all the time. Her life was hard, and every time she was disappointed, she would say it, sometimes mumbling it, sometimes almost shouting, often laughing, in spite of her bad luck. Then strangely, the Dominicans had the same expression. I was so shocked the first time I heard it and understood it. The same fatalism, the same willingness to accept whatever had happened. Perhaps that's why they welcomed us. Perhaps that's why I felt so at home there. Who knows?

I had planned so well for that day. I was to have my revenge, finally. Everything was set. It had been a difficult few months. Seeing Vargas every day. He breathed, laughed, ate, made love. How many, including Anabela, José and Nereida, had he deprived of the pleasures of living? I would finally exact justice, a justice we were denied in Santo Domingo. It was providence. Surely, fate, or perhaps just chance had brought him to us. Did it really matter? We would make him admit what he had done, and then we would take retribution. But at that moment, there was a ripple in the universe. Something intervened. I would have killed him with my own hands. Instead, he died by someone else's, and I knew this curse that followed me and visited itself on everyone I loved. It had touched yet another. In any event, the bastard was dead."

Tolya put the sheet of paper on the desk and sat down on its edge.

"He so much as says it," Pete said.

"I agree. Hard to believe."

"We need to know the truth, exactly as it happened."

"We can confront Erno directly…"

"I don't think he'll change his story."

There was a knock on the door.

"Come in," said Pete.

It was Loretta, the Captain's secretary. "Can you come into the Captain's office, please?"

"Sure," Tolya said. "What's up?"

"I don't know. He said he wants to see you."

Tolya and Pete followed Loretta down the hall into the Captain's office. "Yes, Cap?" Tolya said.

"I just received a call from Rabbi Shalom Rothman. It seems your prime suspect, Henrique Hierron, is dead. I think this investigation is over."

Both Tolya and Pete were momentarily stunned by the captain's news. Tolya dropped into the chair in front of the captain's desk "That's just too sad. And we're almost there."

The Captain placed his hands over his eyes. "Not to be crass gentlemen, but seriously, I humored you guys long enough. There's no reason to continue with this. We have a confession in a forty-year-old murder. The confessed killer just died. And you've decided you might have an alternate suspect? Like I said, this case is closed. The funeral is tomorrow morning in Jersey. Loretta has the information. If you feel you want to go for closure, I'm okay with that. But when you get back, I want you to close the files on this. They will be on my desk by the next morning."

Tolya closed the door as Pete sat down at his side of the desk. He picked up the laser pointer and circled the photo Tolya had pinned to the board just before Loretta interrupted them. "You really think he did this?"

"Yes, I do. But it was an accident. Think about it. The bullet holes in the wainscoting. The effort they went to covering up. The entry Max wrote, and in a secret diary in a language he believed no one else who would come across it could read. And he skirts the issue in the diary. No names, nothing overt that could connect anyone to the crime."

"What about Max's wife? They were from the same place. She might have spoken Slovak."

"But she wasn't aware of the crime."

"True."

"And if she did know, if she did find out, she would want to protect him too. She would never say a word."

"Do you think she knew?"

Pete shrugged. "Who knows? They covered their tracks really well. They were clever. We'll never know."

"They had to be to have survived what they did. And besides, people see what they want to see and turn away when they don't want to know."

"At this point it doesn't really matter. If she knew she never let on and now, well, she's been dead for years. What do you want to do?"

"I'm not sure there's anything we can do. You heard the Captain."

"Yeah, I heard him brother, but I know you. You gonna let this thing go? You ready to move on?"

"I'm ready to go to the funeral, and then decide. You?"

Pete smiled. "I'm not as attached to these two old guys as you. But sometimes I feel like you feel, like you're channeling old Max, like somehow you think he needs you to see his point of view, to justify what he did."

Tolya laughed. "Sometimes I do feel like that. I get that old man. He seems like a guy with a curse, everyone he touched ended up dead or ruined, but I don't believe that. I think he was dealt some really bad hands, kinda like me, and he needed people to understand he tried to do the best he could, kinda like me. And you? You ready to walk away?"

"Yeah, for me it was different. I needed to know what happened down there in my country, the truth, what my people did in those days. That interview with the Tejada's was it for me. I have to accept it. What that man did to my country destroyed it. He took paradise and turned it into hell. I'm ashamed, but at least now I know. If my mother were still alive, I'd have some questions for her. I'm gonna ask my aunts and uncles and maybe they're gonna tell me the truth, but yeah, I'm ready to move on."

"Brother, I wanna say one more thing."

"What's that?" Pete smiled knowing full well what was coming. He also knew Tolya knew how much he hated sentimental shit. But he loved Tolya like a brother, so he was gonna let him slide, just a little.

"What I learned from all this is that Max couldn't have survived the things he did without Erno. And I wouldn't be me today without you."

Pete smiled. He'd hold the hard time he would normally give Tolya for saying that for another day. "Thanks, brotherman," he said. "Same goes for me."

Chapter 26

Washington Heights, NYC
18 August 2008
1:15 p.m.

S halom eased himself into his chair. He turned to the window. The old house on 187th street was completely gone now, as was everyone and everything that had ever been connected to it. Now that he had buried Erno—which was no easy thing—he had to begin anew. Erno was the last link to Shalom's past, the last person on earth who still referred to him as Stephen. In some way, everything that had happened in the past couple weeks now made sense. It was an end and a beginning.

The funeral was a lonely affair, but then everyone else who might have known Erno was dead, save the son of a distant cousin who lived in Philadelphia. Shalom had met him many years earlier at some family affair. Unexpectedly, perhaps even uncomfortably, the two detectives had shown up. Shalom welcomed them with a nod as he prayed silently over the coffin.

Shalom wondered why he was doing it. Erno was a confirmed atheist. He recalled the discussion his parents had with Ava and Erno about their burial plots. He could hear them clucking away in Hungarian as he completed his homework in his bedroom down the hall from their living room. Had his mother agreed to cremation he wouldn't be standing here right now. She couldn't and had convinced them all that after what the Germans had done to their families, the Jewish religious prohibition against cremation was not the point, the ovens of Auschwitz were. There must be evidence that they lived and died. Regardless of what they might have believed personally about god, the soul, life after death. Cremation would be a victory for the Nazis. When Ava agreed, Max and Erno relented. And so, Shalom found himself praying over a man who never mumbled a word of praise for god in any language in his entire life, in an Orthodox Jewish cemetery in New Jersey.

Standing there in the cemetery in that plot, his parents, Ava, and Erno at his feet, he came to the forgiveness he had sought for so long. He also realized that he forgave his former self, Stephen Redmond. But there were things this self, Shalom Rothman, had done badly and he needed to make good on those things. Mostly, they pertained to his son and his wife. He had to find a way for them to become a family again. He could no longer make believe nothing had happened. Rachel was in prison and Baruch needed her, regardless of where she was. He had forgiven her long ago for what had put her there, but that forgiveness was empty if he let Baruch forget her. It was time to bring Baruch to his mother.

෴

Rachel waited patiently in her cell for the prison matron to come to fetch her for her visit with Shalom. Shalom said he had a surprise for her. She appreciated his small gestures.

In the first few months after she went to prison, she could barely look at Shalom, let alone touch him or let him touch her. She was too riddled with guilt. As a married couple, they were permitted a private room. She blushed even now at the thought of what the private room with its single bed and thin mattress were provided for. When she learned the term from the other inmates, conjugal visit, she blushed even more deeply. Those moments were the most intimate of her life. She would never consider spoiling them in the glare of the fluorescent fixture that cast its harsh light on the cold, antiseptic room they were provided by the State of New York. Intimacy would wait until they were reunited in their home.

She marveled still at the strength of Shalom's character. Even after what she had done, he stood by her. He could have demanded a *get*. The *Beit Din* would have granted it without question. Instead he took her in his arms and comforted her. After her arrest, even when the defense attorney had suggested they try to get an acquittal based on her psychological state, Shalom stood by her. It was her decision, he said. She felt she had done enough wrong. She had to accept responsibility. Hiding it, covering it up, had only made her more insane than the act itself. She pleaded to involuntary manslaughter and would serve a minimum five-year sentence.

Her sole regret was leaving Baruch. Her heart broke every time she thought of him. She has nursed him and protected him. Now she felt as if she had abandoned him.

She had no idea what he made of her absence, or how he would react to her when she finally returned to them. She feared he was irrevocably lost to her.

Rachel knelt slightly in front of the mirror over the sink in her cell and brushed out her wig. She straightened her collar and stood by the door waiting for the guard. She had something to discuss with Shalom.

ഗ∞ഗ

Shalom waited with Baruch in the anteroom of the prison. Baruch had been surprisingly easy to handle on the trip up from the city. He sat quietly with his book in the back seat. Every so often Shalom peered into the rear-view mirror to find Baruch either contentedly reading or sleeping.

The drive took about three hours. When they arrived, Shalom explained to Baruch that they would have to go through a security checkpoint. He wanted to keep him calm. The metal detectors and the gloved, prying, hands of the guards could be enough to send him into a panic. The prison had arranged for a special aide, someone with experience with autism to shepherd Baruch through. It went well. There was a moment when Shalom thought Baruch might fall apart. The guard separated him momentarily from his basketball. It was back in his hands quickly enough to avoid a catastrophe. Now they waited in silence for a prison matron to escort them to the room where they would see Rachel.

Shalom realized the moment had come. He had to explain to Baruch what was about to happen. In the nearly two years since Rachel was incarcerated, he had learned, because he had to, how to guide Baruch, how to speak to him.

"Baruch," he said. Baruch turned his head. Shalom smiled. Baruch smiled back, as if on cue. "Son, I know this will be surprising for you. You remember how you used to ask me for *eema* all the time?"

Baruch looked at Shalom, his eyes fixed on Shalom's face, but at the same time not focused on anything in particular. That was the thing with autism. It was so difficult, really impossible, to read what Baruch was thinking.

"We are here to see *eema*." He searched Baruch's face for some sense of understanding. There was none.

"Mr. Rothman?" a voice called. A large woman was half hidden by the door.

"Yes," Shalom replied.

"Follow me, please."

Shalom took his hat from his lap and put it on. He rose and took Baruch gently by his left arm. "All right, son, let's go." They walked through the heavy door into a hallway, Baruch carrying his basketball in both hands. He walked heavily, slightly bent in a defensive position against the unfamiliar environment. Far off, the muffled sounds of shouting could be heard, though the words were not identifiable.

At the end of the hallway the prison matron unlocked the door to a small meeting room marked conjugal visits. Shalom blushed, as he always did, when he saw that sign. The matron pushed open the door slowly. Rachel sat in the chair at the far end of the room. Behind her was another door that led into the woman's prison.

When Rachel saw the door open, she stood. When she saw Baruch behind Shalom she collapsed back into the chair immediately. Her breath caught in her throat. Tears welled up in her eyes. She forced herself up again on wobbly knees.

"Hello, my darling," said Shalom.

Baruch came into the room. He stopped for a moment and looked at Rachel in a different way than he had looked at Shalom only moments before. The focus and recognition that were missing were now clearly there. He stopped for a moment. His basketball dropped to the floor. He took two tentative steps toward Rachel. She moved forward covering the few feet between them.

Baruch's mouth and eyes were wide open. He reached out to touch Rachel and she did the same. They lowered themselves onto the cot provided by the state for a very different kind of intimacy. Baruch wrapped his arms around Rachel and placed his head on her right shoulder. She embraced him, placed her cheek against the top of his head and whispered, "My son. I thought you would forget me." She looked up at Shalom, the tears falling from her eyes. "Thank you," she said.

After a long while Baruch let go. He and Rachel sat next to each other on the cot. Shalom sat on the chair by the door at the rear of the room. The harsh fluorescent light above them blanketed coldness onto the warm scene like snow on a golden autumn landscape.

"Ask him what that is," Shalom said to Rachel, pointing at the basketball, which had settled into the corner of the room by the door.

Rachel looked at him. "Why?"

"Just ask him."

She took Baruch's hand in hers again. "What did you bring with you?"

Baruch sat up straight and smiled broadly. "Ball," he exclaimed.

Rachel was shocked. She hadn't heard Baruch speak a word that clearly since just after his third birthday. "Where, how, when?" she asked.

Shalom hesitated for a moment. All this time and he still hadn't told Rachel about Carlos. "At the school," he said. "The other day when I went to pick him up, they told me. Then he told me."

"That's remarkable," Rachel said. The tears welled up in her eyes again.

"Carlos," said Baruch with the same look of glee he had on his face when he said ball.

Rachel looked at Shalom. "What did he say?"

Shalom was equally as shocked. He hadn't expected that. "I'm not sure," he answered, though he knew full well what he'd heard.

"Carlos," Baruch said again.

Rachel looked a Shalom. "It sounded like Carlos?"

"Well, it may be," Shalom replied. There was no point in hiding it any longer. "I needed help. I couldn't handle him alone, and neither could María."

"I don't understand," Rachel said.

"You remember Carlos, the boy who worked afternoons with my father?"

There was no way Rachel could forget him. "Of course." She hesitated for a long moment. "I treated him very badly."

"He's helping me with Baruch. He takes care of him after school and sometimes on Sundays."

Rachel trembled. Would this crime never leave her? Reminders were everywhere, from her incarceration to the reappearance of one of the principal characters in the drama. She had to learn to forgive, especially herself. "*Baruch HaShem*," she said.

Chapter 27

Washington Heights, NYC
20 August 2008
1:15 p.m.

Tolya signed off on the report closing the case of the mummy in the wall of 669 West 187th Street. He handed it to Pete for counter signing.

"There you go, bro. Done. Here are copies of the summaries on the two cases the Captain handed me this morning. We should get started on them right away."

Tolya looked over the two pages. "One of these is a series of break-ins, and the other is a run-away. I thought we're homicide detectives."

Pete smiled. "I guess they didn't find any bodies this past couple of weeks."

Tolya picked up his gun, placed it into its holster and slipped his cell into his pants pocket.

"Where you going?"

"I'm gonna drop these off at the Captain's office."

"You need your gun and your cell for that?"

"I've got an appointment."

"With who?"

"Rabbi Rothman."

Pete rolled his eyes. "I thought we're done with this?"

"He called me."

Pete smiled. "Okay. Finish it off, brotherman, then let's bury it, finally, for good."

Tolya climbed the two flights to Shalom's office and knocked lightly on the door. Shalom's secretary answered and led him directly into Shalom's office. Shalom stood and offered his hand to Tolya. "Thanks for coming, detective."

"You're welcome, Rabbi."

Shalom pointed to the chair. "Please, sit down."

"What did you want to see me about?"

"First of all, I wanted to thank you for coming to Erno's funeral. I can tell you there's really nothing sadder than burying someone alone. Occasionally, I have to do it. Everyone else is gone, they didn't have any children. It's a very lonely experience."

"Well, Detective Gonzalvez and I felt we needed to be there. We got to know Erno pretty well. I'm sure it was very hard for you."

"It was. In many ways Erno was like a second father to me. As you know, my father was not the easiest person, and sadly, not the best parent."

"As we've spoken previously, neither was mine."

"I've come to forgive mine for that."

"I can't say that I've come that far yet."

"I hope you will. It makes a real difference."

An awkward silence blanketed the room. Shalom hesitated, not sure he wanted to continue telling Tolya why he had asked to see him. He steeled his resolve and took a deep breath. "That's not why I asked to see you, though. I have something I want to share with you."

"What's that?"

"The conversation I had with Erno, the night before he died."

Tolya leaned forward in the chair. "Really, please tell me."

"I should tell you first that this whole incident…"

"What incident?"

"The discovery of that body in the walls of my father's old rooming house, the investigation into it, caught me quite by surprise. It unbalanced me. Dredged up a lot of bad memories, and eventually the truth."

"Really." Tolya knew now that he and Pete were right. "What exactly?" He wanted to hear it. He wanted to hear Shalom's truth directly from Shalom.

"I was very unsettled when you and your partner came here a couple weeks back. Your questions felt too close, too intimate. I felt like you were dragging me back to a place I had escaped from, no, run away from. But I couldn't remember. I didn't want to remember. I beg you to understand. My wife is in prison, my son has his problems as you well know, and I'm alone. No parents, no siblings, no one."

Tolya knew that feeling. But he had Karin at home, and Pete all day. Shalom, he knew, was alone, adrift.

"All I have is this community. Your questions were dragging me back to a life I had forsaken years ago. I wanted to be left alone. But something was nagging at me. Honestly, I told you I didn't remember, and for the most part I didn't. That was the truth. I lied though about a couple of things. I apologize for that. I did remember the victim, and he was an evil man, that I can tell you. More so than you know."

"I do know," Tolya said.

Shalom was so deep in his thoughts though that Tolya knew his reply didn't register. "And I felt like I knew more than I actually could remember," Shalom his eyes focused on the vista outside the window where the old houses had stood till a week ago. "The night before Erno died, I went to see him. I demanded to know the truth. I had gone to see a therapist and she walked me through my memories. I needed Erno to confirm what I recalled."

"And did he?"

"In his way, yes."

"And what did you remember?"

Shalom sat up in his chair. He took a deep breath and then exhaled slowly. "It was me, or should I say, it was my fault. I shot Vargas."

"Are you sure of that?"

"Yes."

"Can you tell me what happened?"

"Of course." Shalom hesitated a moment, caught in his memories. "I was at my friend's apartment on Audubon Avenue. I was twelve. It was the fourth of July, the day after my birthday. I was walking home just after the fireworks in Highbridge Park. As I was passing the rooming house, I heard screaming. The lights were on. It was my father's voice. But I thought my parents were at a party at their friend's apartment up on Fort Washington Avenue. I went up to the house and when I opened the door, there was a fight going on. Erno and Vargas were wrestling. Vargas had a gun and it was pointed at my father. He dropped the gun accidentally. It slid across the floor in my direction." Shalom stopped for a moment and took another breath. "I picked it up. I was confused and frightened. I pointed it at Vargas and screamed at him to let go of Erno. They were all so shocked to hear my voice that they stopped fighting and looked at me. I was shaking and began screaming myself, and I remember now that I was crying. Erno came toward me, his hand outstretched demanding the gun. I raised it again and it went off twice. I dropped it, and when it hit the floor it went off again. At least one of the shots, I don't know which, hit Vargas. The blood was everywhere. I became hysterical. I remember my father screaming at him, he said, 'first Anabela and my unborn child, now my son, you've destroyed us once again, wasn't one child enough!' I felt a stinging pain across my face, I know now that was Erno slapping me to calm me down. After that I don't remember anything till the next day when my father came to talk to me."

"What did he say to you?"

"Not much. He asked me questions to determine how much I remembered. It wasn't much. He told me to forget whatever I thought I saw, that I should never tell my mother anything, that it was our secret, a father and son, and that no one could ever come between us or hurt us again. And so, I did as he instructed, but in the end the lingering memory drove me away from him, not to him."

"Thank you for telling me."

"Detective,"

"Tolya, please,"

"Tolya, if you want to arrest me, I understand. I did a terrible thing. I took a man's life…"

"He was a very terrible man."

"Nonetheless, I killed him."

"Rabbi…Shalom, if I may call you that,"

"Of course, please,"

"This man was a murderer, and not just of your father's friend and girlfriend. He was one of Trujillo's henchmen. We interviewed members of his family during our investigation and they confirmed for us how vicious and evil he was. If your father hadn't planned his murder, someone else would have."

Shalom hesitated. "Planned his murder?"

"Yes."

"How do you know that?"

"Erno, and it was confirmed by your father's diaries."

"His diaries?"

"Yes. You never claimed them from evidence after your father's murder investigation ended. As to arresting you, well the case is already closed. We have a signed confession from Erno."

"I don't want his memory sullied like that. He was devoted to my father. He doesn't deserve to be remembered as a murderer."

"Sadly, as you yourself said, there is no one left to remember him, except us. Everyone else is gone. And we know the truth. And besides, I don't see what value arresting you for an accidental death nearly forty years ago of a man who deserved far worse would serve."

Shalom exhaled. "Thank you…Tolya."

"You're welcome, Shalom." Tolya picked up the large paper shopping bag he had brought with him from the floor beside him. "If you would like to know the whole story, here are your father's diaries. We don't need them. This might help you to heal. Read them. He was quite a man, your father. He made mistakes, but he had a huge heart, and he went through things that would have killed a lesser man. He was very strong."

"Thank you."

Tolya rose to leave. He shook Shalom's hand and smiled. "We're not that different. You and I," he said. "We're both the sons of larger than life fathers who didn't know how to communicate with us. And because of this we seek the truth, always, in our own ways."

As Tolya left and closed the door Shalom sat down and took the first of the volumes from the bag. He opened it. His father's flowery European cursive filled the pages. The entry was dated July 3, 1954, Shalom's birth date. It was written in English. Shalom read the words out loud, "Finally, I have a son!"

When Pete arrived at the Monkey Bar, Tolya was already on his second beer. He waved to the bartender. "I'll have what he's having."

"You want the shot of vodka too?"

He looked at the empty shot glass. "Boy, this is gonna be good. No, make mine tequila."

The bartender brought the beer and the shot and placed it in front of Pete. He downed the shot quickly then took a swig from the bottle of Corona. "Well, what's this urgent thing you have to tell me?"

"We were right. He did it."

"Shalom killed him?"

"Yeah, well, accidently, sort of." Tolya explained the series of events from that long-ago Independence Day as Shalom had related them to him an hour earlier.

"Do you wanna arrest him?" Pete said, smiling.

Tolya clinked the neck of his beer bottle against both sides of Pete's. "No. It was accidental. But we were right. Here's to us."

Pete tapped the neck of his bottle against both sides of Tolya's again. "There's not a case we can't solve, brother-man. Even one that's been around longer than we have."

Epilogue
Washington Heights, NYC
Sept 14, 2008
11:15 a.m.

Karin lay in bed at Columbia Presbyterian Hospital, sweaty but happy. She held the seven pound., twenty-inch baby boy in her arms. He had one eye open. "My beautiful baby. My beautiful little Oleg."

"Not so fast," Pete said. He tipped his head toward Tolya, sitting on the edge of the bed. "He didn't tell you?"

Tolya chuckled.

"I thought we made a decision?" said Karin. I thought you wanted to name him after your brother?"

"I've got another name."

"What?"

"I've been thinking about it for a while. I just didn't tell you."

"But you told your partner over there? Wait a minute, when he carries your child around for nine months, you can tell him first."

"I wasn't sure. I needed to bounce it off someone."

Karin sighed. "All right then, let's have it."

Tolya looked at Pete and smiled.

"Go ahead, brotherman."

"Erno."

Karin wrinkled her brow. "Erno? After Max's friend?"

"He was more than Max's friend. He was his brother..."

"...From another mother," said Pete.

"Kinda like us," Tolya said, looking at Pete.

"But you have someone to name him for."

"And we might have more children."

"Not happening," said Karin. She stroked the baby's forehead gently.

"We'll see," Tolya replied. Pete bumped his fist.

"Maybe with Pete, over there," Karin said. "This shop is closed."

"We can discuss that another time."

"Why Erno, Tol?" Karin asked.

"He had nobody but Max. He's gone and there's no one to remember him."

"Oleg's gone too."

"But I remember him. If we don't have more kids, we might have grandchildren. That will never happen for Erno. He was a good man. The world should remember him. And besides, every Max should have an Erno." Tolya smiled at Pete.

"Kiss your bride, sentimental fool," Pete said

Tolya leaned over Karin and kissed her. He lingered there for a moment then kissed her again. He took Erno from her arms into his and sat back down on the edge of the bed. "And thank you, my darling."

"For what?"

"For loving me."

THE END

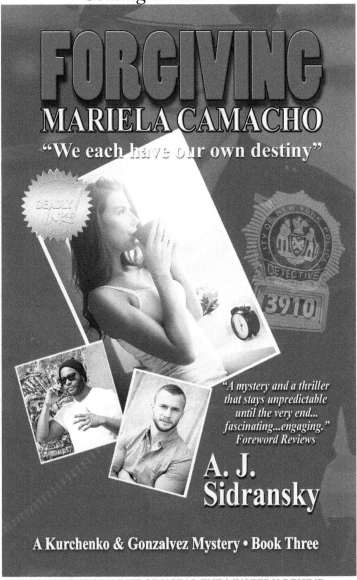

Coming Winter 2021

FORGIVING
MARIELA CAMACHO
"We each have our own destiny"

"A mystery and a thriller that stays unpredictable until the very end... fascinating...engaging."
Foreword Reviews

A. J. Sidransky

A Kurchenko & Gonzalvez Mystery • Book Three

BONUS SHORT STORY INTRODUCING THE MYSTERY BEHIND
FORGIVING MARIELA CAMACHO.

Dead Men Don't Hammer Nails

Tel Aviv, Israel,
a Friday evening
May 1995

"Inspector, she left a note," said an exasperator Captain Alon. "I don't see any reason for us to initiate an investigation into a suicide. This is an open and shut case. And besides, she was a prostitute."

"We don't know that for sure."

"She says it in her note."

Detective Ari ben-Shimon felt the anger rise in his chest. "No one cuts their own throat, especially not like that." He jumped out of the chair, his palms landing on the edge of the Captain's desk. "I doubt she would even know how to build such a thing."

"Perhaps her pimp built it for her?" Alon replied. He dropped the case file into the box at his feet.

"That's an insult," growled Detective Mustafa Kemal. He walked to the window, his fists clenched, his back to the Captain. "You don't want to pursue this because she was Arab, not because she was a prostitute."

Alon shifted in his chair. "Do you think you could look at me when you speak to me?"

Kemal cringed. He turned slowly in the Captain's direction.

"You really believe I feel that way?"

"No sir, sorry." A forced smile concealed Kemal's anger. "I have to stress what Ari said. We examined the crime scene thoroughly. Note or no note, this was no suicide."

Alon picked up his phone. That was his signal to end the conversation. "We have other things to do gentlemen, beside disproving a suicide note."

Ben-Shimon challenged him again. "What about the partial print?" He figured one more shot was worth it, a lesson every Israeli boy learned early on in his military service.

"It's probably hers," replied Alon.

Three Hours Earlier

The old apartment building on Kibbutz Galuyot Street in the southern reaches of Tel Aviv near where the city merges with Jaffa dated to the early 1960's. Never particularly desirable, the neighborhood was poorer than ever and becoming poorer still. The building's poured concrete exterior was dirty and pockmarked from age and lack of maintenance. Across the street was a dusty, sandy, park in a similar state of disrepair. Old women sat on the broken wooden benches gossiping loudly in a mixture of Russian, Hebrew and other languages neither ben-Shimon nor Kemal could identify, a common occurrence since the arrival of a million former Soviet citizens a few years earlier. Two old men sat at a chess table intently staring at their pieces and spitting shells from sunflower seeds like bullets at the pavement.

Ben-Shimon and Kemal pushed through the crowd that had gathered in front of the building. They flashed their badges, entering the dusty common hallway. A uniformed policeman stood in front of the door leading to the basement storage room.

They waited for their eyes to adjust to the light level. Inside the dark, musty room was a horrific scene. The elaborate frame of a bizarre structure nearly filled the abandoned space. Seated in a chair suspended from the frame was the body of a woman, naked, a pool of congealing blood on the concrete floor under her glistening in the semi-darkness. Her throat had been cut cleanly, a long, sharp, kitchen knife dangling from a thin leather strap attached to her right wrist. A complicated pulley system stood sentinel behind the seat.

They didn't know exactly when the woman's violent end had come, though the still partially liquid state of the blood indicated it had happened within past 24 hours. A terrified call from a screaming woman whose children had wandered into the usually locked storage room had summoned them in the hours just before Shabbat.

Kemal covered his mouth and nose with his hand. He gagged slightly. "I've never seen anything like that before."

"The victim or the structure?" said ben-Shimon. He breathed in the fetid air, apparently unaffected by the sight or smell. No amount of carnage could shock him after what he'd seen as a young soldier in Lebanon, some fifteen years earlier.

"Either and both," replied Kemal.

"You'll take the photos?" ben-Shimon asked.

"*Bivadai.*"

Ben-Shimon slipped on a pair of rubber gloves and walked slowly around the strange structure that dominated the room. He inspected the pulley system suspended within it. Nailed to the center post was a piece of paper. Ben-Shimon carefully slipped it through the nail and unfolded it. The writing was slightly smudged and in Arabic. "Mustafa, look at this," he said.

Kemal slung the camera over his shoulder. He shined ben-Shimon's flashlight onto the paper.

"I ask Allah for forgiveness, I cannot live this life any longer. I have made myself a whore. I have dishonored my family. I have sinned before Allah. To save my family from my shame I take my own life. Please forgive me. Laila."

"A suicide?" said ben-Shimon. "No way."

"Not possible, it's haram," said Kemal. He gazed at the small, delicate body covered in blood. "How could she have built this?" He turned to ben-Shimon. "Why would she have built this?"

Ben-Shimon walked back to the door and pulled the fingerprint kit from his bag. "Let's see what we find." He dusted the wood beams that held up the structure and the pulleys suspended from it. They would dust the knife later, though he doubted anyone else's prints beside the victim's would be there. He shined his flashlight on the structure looking for prints. One appeared on the left post. "Mustafa, take a look here."

"It looks like a thumb. Too big to be hers."

Ben-Shimon lifted the print carefully then placed the adhesive tape on a lift card and stored it gently in an evidence bag. "Perhaps her suicide was assisted?"

Kemal didn't respond. He stood in front of the dead woman, staring at her yet averting his eyes at the same time. Ben-Shimon scanned the rest of the structure for more prints but found none. "Do you have all the photos we need?"

"For now."

"Let's go speak to the woman who called it in. The evidence team can finish up here later," said ben-Shimon. He pulled out his pager and sent a message to the station, then called to the uniformed cop standing at the front door of the building. "Where is the woman who phoned in the case?"

"In her apartment." He pointed to the door at the second-floor landing.

Ben-Shimon and Kemal climbed the one flight then knocked. A woman appeared as the door opened. She stared at Kemal.

"Shabbat Shalom," ben-Shimon said. "Excuse me, could we speak with you for a moment?" He pulled his badge from his pocket as did Kemal.

"It's nearly Shabbat," she said in broken, Russian-accented Hebrew. "I have to prepare." She looked Kemal up and down again.

"We only need a moment," said Kemal, his Hebrew perfect.

The woman was un-phased. "I've already told the first officer I don't know anything. My daughters found the door open and went inside. You saw what they found. They're in their rooms now, being punished for going in there to begin with. I didn't hear anything except them screaming. When I went to see what was wrong I found that," she pointed toward the basement, "I called the police." Someone called out to her from inside the apartment in Russian. "I'm sorry, I have to go now. She was a *kurva* anyway. She got what she deserved. If her people had caught her, they would have done much worse."

Ben-Shimon glanced at Kemal. He saw the look of anger in Mustafa's eyes. Ben-Shimon shook his head almost imperceptibly, Kemal catching his meaning immediately and maintaining his composure. "What do you mean her people?"

The woman looked at Kemal again. "She was Arab. One could tell."

Ben-Shimon wasn't sure how. The victim was naked, dead and bloodied from an open gash on her throat. He thought to ask but reconsidered. He wanted to end the conversation for Mustafa's sake. He and Kemal had known each other since they were eleven years old. He knew, as a Jew, that his world was different from Mustafa's, an Arab.

"Thank you," ben-Shimon said. "Here are our cards. Please call us if you can think of anything else that might help."

Kemal and ben-Shimon walked out of the building into the late afternoon sunlight. The crowd had dissipated. The park across the street was empty. "Keep guard on the crime scene till the evidence team leaves then padlock it," ben-Shimon said to the uniformed officer.

Kemal looked at ben-Shimon and let out his breath slowly. "Hers was a human life too."

"I know." Ben-Shimon pulled a pack of cigarettes from his coat and slipped one between his lips. He fumbled in his pants for a match, looked around and shook his head. "What do you want me to say. These Russians have a different view of life than we do." He dragged deeply on the cigarette. "Does this place look familiar to you, the park, not the building?"

Kemal thought for a moment then looked down the street. "Yes, I didn't realize when we got here. Two or three buildings down. Yes, over there," he said, "that building."

"Remember that Russian? The case about the Philippine woman?"

Kemal nodded his head. "Her throat was cut too."

The Next Day

The station was particularly quiet on Shabbat. There was a skeleton staff manning the phone and a couple of officers on duty in case of emergencies. In a country with little violent crime, there was little need for a full staff at a police station on Israel's weekly day off.

"*Boker tov*," said the duty officer to ben-Shimon and Kemal as they entered the stationhouse.

"*Boker tov*," they responded. They had decided to pursue the investigation, despite the Captain's objections.

"It's not your weekend," she said. "Did you check the schedule?"

Ben-Shimon didn't reply. She was nosy and a gossip. That was her way of asking them why they were there. He smiled at her and continued down the hall, Kemal at his side, silent as well. "Close the door," he said as they entered their office. "I don't like her snooping around."

Mustafa laughed. "You need to relax, she's harmless." He slipped the door shut almost silently. "Did you send out the print for analysis last night?"

"Yes, I put a rush request on it. It will be at least two weeks though."

The evidence box from the case of the Filipina woman was tucked under Kemal's desk. He'd placed it there the evening before. He pulled it out, put it on top of the desk, took out the file and sat down facing Ari. Kemal read silently for a moment then took the photograph of the suspect and placed it on the desk. "I remember him clearly now. He was very creepy."

Ari nodded. "Yes, a real slimy guy. What was his name?"

"Natan Hayat. A Russian."

"Remind me, why did we drop the case?"

Mustafa thumbed through the report. He stopped at the last paragraph of the last page. "Due to lack of any hard evidence to implicate any specific suspect, the presiding officer has instructed that the case is to be closed and filed as unsolved."

Ben-Shimon thought for a moment. "What year was that?"

"1993."

They both knew who the presiding officer was, and he wasn't interested in cases involving Israel's growing population of guest workers. 'She was probably involved in something illegal,' ben-Shimon recalled him saying.

"Perhaps we should take a trip over to the park and find out what happened to Mr. Hayat. See if he's still around. I think I'd like to chat with him again."

Kemal closed the file and placed the box back under his desk. "Do you think we should wait till after Shabbat?"

Ben-Shimon shook his head. "No, not in that neighborhood. Those people aren't observant. They just use it as an excuse."

****

Kemal and ben-Shimon walked into the dusty park and sat down on one of the benches. The wooden slats of the seat were chipped and uncomfortable. The park was filled with people, more than it could comfortably hold. Many brought their own chairs, less uncomfortable than the bench Kemal and ben-Shimon sat on. The locals stared at them.

"Why don't we try those women over there, by the swings?" said Kemal.

"I was thinking the old men playing chess."

"No, the women are more likely to talk."

"All right. Let's go," said ben-Shimon.

They approached the women, a group of four surrounded by a dozen children. Though they wrapped their hair in scarves and wore longish skirts, their short sleeve blouses with their low necklines showed too much cleavage for them to be religious.

"*Selicha*," ben-Shimon said. They flashed their badges. "*Shabbat shalom.*"

"*Shabbat shalom*," one woman replied. Three of them stood with their arms crossed against their chests. "If you're here about the murdered woman, we don't know anything."

A child, a small girl, tugged at her skirt. "Eema, I need to go potty," she said. The woman bent down and put her hands on both the child's cheeks. "Okay, Gali will take you." She called to another child by the swings, perhaps ten years old. "Take Leah, please. She needs the *sherut*."

Kemal pulled the photo of Hayat from his pocket. "Do you know this man?"

The women looked at the photo and nodded. "Yes, yes. He used to live with his family over there," one of the women said. She pointed to a building across the street from the park.

"Used to live?" ben-Shimon asked.

"They moved away about a year and a half ago."

"Did you know him or the family well?"

The women looked at each other. One smirked. "No," she said. "They were very unfriendly."

"They didn't like us, looked down on us," another said. The women exchanged looks again. "They were from Moscow. We are from Samarkand. They thought they were better than us."

"Where did they move to?"

"A settlement in the territories."

"They were religious?"

The women laughed again. "They had an opportunity."

"Has this guy ever returned?" Kemal asked.

The women looked at each other and shook their heads. "No."

Sunday morning

Ben-Shimon called the Ministry of Immigration at 8:30 AM. It took several pass-alongs to arrive at the right person. It seems the Hayat family had become Ba'al T'shuvah, born again Jews. They had returned to the practice of their ancient religion through the guiding hand of the Chabad Lubovitch movement. As a thank you, these impoverished Russian immigrants had been given a house in a new settlement in the territories called Ramat ha'Datim. They'd also never have to work again. The settlement was supported by funds provided by the Chabad so that the men could sit and study Talmud in the heart of Judea all day, every day. Ben-Shimon was consistently amazed by the ability of these people to find a way to milk the system.

But what really shocked him was what had happened to them. About a month earlier the entire family was murdered in a terrorist attack. It was all over the news and of course he and Mustafa had seen the reports but he certainly would never have recalled the family name or the name of the tiny settlement. The suspect was dead.

Ben-Shimon and Kemal went to Alon's office and gave him the news. Alon peered over his reading glasses and smiled. "So, I guess it is in fact a suicide."

Kemal couldn't contain himself. "Captain. You didn't see the crime scene, there's no way. This was murder, a gruesome murder. Whoever did this could do it again."

"Case closed," said Alon. He picked up his phone and punched in his secretary's extension. "Ahava, please get the Government Attorney's office for me."

Ben-Shimon and Kemal took the cue as an order and left the office. Ari had sensed Mustafa was right all along. Since the victim was Arab and likely a prostitute, the easiest thing to do was to accept the suicide note and close the case. And the case was closed by the same presiding officer who closed the investigation into the murder of the Filipina woman two years earlier, Captain Alon.

One Month Later

Ben-Shimon found the envelop on his desk when he arrived. He had pretty much forgotten about it. "Mustafa read this," he said, handing the paper to Kemal.

"The fingerprint belongs to Hayat." said Kemal.

How is that possible? He was dead for a month before we found the woman in that basement."

"The fingerprint matches the one taken when he immigrated from Russia. The expert says it's an exact match."

Ben-Shimon considered the situation for a moment. "We have to tell the Captain."

Kemal laughed. "Really? Because he's going to reopen an investigation based upon a fingerprint coming from a man who was dead a month before the murder? Remember who he is."

"Come on."

Kemal followed ben-Shimon reluctantly down the hall and into Alon's office. The Captain read the one-page report from the fingerprint expert and laughed. "So, this dead man left a fingerprint at a crime scene?"

"It's a 100% match," said ben-Shimon. "Maybe he's not dead?"

The Captain smirked. "Then who was the man found dead in his bed burned alive by terrorists at Ramat ha'Datim? The whole family was murdered by those animals."

Ben-Shimon looked at Mustafa from the corner of his eye, sharing the anger evident on his face. But he knew he had to defuse this. "Perhaps there was a mistake?"

"Israel Military Police doesn't make mistakes. And I'm one hundred percent sure dead men don't hammer nails.

We have a suicide note. Case closed." The Captain reached for his phone. Kemal stared at the Captain, his eyes lingering, his lower lip trembling, then turned and walked slowly from the room.

THE END

About the Author

A. J. Sidransky's works have received much critical praise. ***Forgiving Máximo Rothman,*** was selected as a finalist in Outstanding Debut Fiction in 2013 by The National Jewish Book Awards. Next Generation Indie Book Awards selected ***Stealing a Summer's Afternoon,*** as a finalist for Best Second Novel in 2015. ***Forgiving Mariela Camacho***, his third work, received the David Award, awarded from Deadly Ink! Writer's Conference for Best Mystery of 2015. His next work, ***The Interpreter***, was released March 2020. It was shortlisted by Next Generation Indie Book Awards for Historical Fiction 2020. ***Forgiving Stephen Redmond***, the final chapter in the Forgiving Series, will be released February 2021.

He has published the following stories, ***La Libreta,*** (The Notebook) in Small Axe Salon (on-line), which was also selected as the winner of the Institute of Caribbean Studies short story contest in 2014. ***Mother Knows Best,*** was published as part of an invitation only collection, Noir Nation 5, and ***The Glint of Metal*** which appears in Crime Café Short Story Anthology, will also appear in the upcoming Fictional Café Anthology, both by invitation. ***El Ladron*** (The Thief) was published by Spinetingler Magazine in summer 2017. ***The Just Men of Bennett Avenue*** will appear in Jewish Noir II, a major short story anthology to be released in 2021.

He is currently at work on ***The Intern***, the second installment in the Interpreter series. ***The King of Arroyo Hondo***, a novella that will anchor a collection of short stories about life in the Dominican Republic today, titled ***Becoming Bachata***, will be published sometime in late 2021

A. J. Sidransky lives in Washington Heights in Upper Manhattan with his wife. He is a dyed in the wool New Yorker, born in the Bronx, and a life-long Yankees fan.

Contact info:
A.J. Sidransky
www.ajsidransky.com
aj@ajsidransky.com
alan.sidransky@yahoo.com
@AJSidransky

CPSIA information can be obtained
at www.ICGtesting.com
Printed in the USA
LVHW052304090221
678896LV00003B/167

9 781953 434524